The African Awakening is
continent. This is a messag
who comes to steal, kill, a
abundantly (John 10:10). Raúl makes the biblical case that the message of life must be tied to the Church, wherever it exists. As the African Church continues to grow and awaken, the message of life will powerfully impact the African continent and ripple across the globe.

TJ Addington
Author of *Leading from the Sandbox* and *High Impact Church Boards*
Creator of The Addington Method

In *The African Awakening: Bringing the Message of Life to the World*, my lifelong friend and partner in ministry, Raúl Reyes, delivers a compelling international message regarding one of the primary heartbreaks of our times—abortion. With meticulous on-site research and profound insight, Raúl unveils a profound truth: amidst a world grappling with population decline, Africa is positioned to emerge as a beacon of hope and vitality for the world. This book masterfully illuminates how Africa's increasing population, coupled with the exponential growth of the Church on the continent, will fundamentally reshape global awareness. More than a mere forecast, this resource serves as a clarion call to action, urging us to equip the African Church with the transformative power of biblically grounded sanctity of human life teachings. In doing so, we not only prepare the Church for its pivotal role in the coming era but also pave the way for a profound movement where African Christians, armed with the message of Christ and the sanctity of life, become catalysts for renewal and redemption across the globe. A must-read for anyone passionate about the intersection of faith, demographics, and the future of humanity.

Pat Layton
Leader, Speaker, Coach
Author of *Surrendering the Secret: Healing the Heartbreak of Abortion*

I have known and labored alongside my brother Raúl Reyes for nearly two decades. Raúl and his wife have been revolutionary resources in the hands of God for nearly forty years in the global mission field created by abortion. Raúl is one of the most culturally sensitive people from Western culture that I have had the privilege of working with in training pastors here in Africa. In this book, Raúl is speaking not only from well-documented data and personal experience, but from a wealth of knowledge gained through his many authentic relationships with ministry leaders across Africa. Africa is truly at a turning point—from a mission field to a mission force. This eye-opening resource will turn your heart toward God's heart for the nations from a very unique perspective and hopefully help you to respond to God's invitation to become part of His movement for life in Africa. For every ministry leader in Africa, this message is right from God's heart. To all who are outside Africa but are involved with equipping and mobilizing the Church in Africa for the advancement of the Gospel on this so-called final stretch, this book cannot be ignored.

Bramuel Musya
Global Movement Leader, Africa

Raúl's decades of leadership in the pregnancy-help movement has been with one foot in the U.S. and the other ministering abroad. In *The African Awakening*, he recalls the chilling insight that "demography is destiny" and envisions the historical strength of the African community catalyzed by the Gospel of Life into global leadership against the culture of death. Championing life has never been more important than in the struggle between the forces of darkness and the agents of life.

Jor-El Godsey
President and CEO
Heartbeat International

As I read through Raúl Reyes' new book, *The African Awakening*, I thought of the many conversations that Raúl and I have had over the years. I consider Raúl a dear friend, one whom God has used to minister and mentor and allow me to partner with him in his clear passion for the sanctity of life. As a pastor, our church is proud to partner with Life Equip Global. I truly believe that this book will be an incredible and much needed resource in the hands of pastors and Church leaders all over the world. He has a gift for clearly laying out and identifying the challenges the Church faces in this spiritual battle that we are in and showing us how to let God work through us to accomplish the mission He has called us to.

Scotty Vaughn
Senior Pastor
Church on the Ranch, Colorado Springs, CO

In *The African Awakening*, I love that Raúl addresses the abortion issue comprehensively. He stresses the centrality of a Gospel-centric response as well as the importance of God's design for marriage, motherhood, and fatherhood as key to stemming the tide of abortion in Africa and beyond. This is certainly the perspective that is needed.

Roland C. Warren
President and CEO
Care Net

The African Awakening is an excellent resource for churches, individuals, and ministries that have a desire to protect unborn children and their mothers. It is a thorough and thoughtful analysis of the problem of abortion in Africa, its beginnings, and the solution. A combination of accurate information, moving testimonies, and focus on Scripture make it a must-read.

Melissa Heiland
Founder and Executive Director, Beautiful Feet International
Author of *A Mother's Comfort*, *A Mother's Journey*, *No Shame* and *Get Set*

In the book *The African Awakening*, my dear friend Raúl has brought to a sharp focus Africa's role in fulfilling God's redemptive plan for all of creation. God has always used Africa to save lives, and in this book, Raúl presents this reality in a simple and more forceful way by highlighting God's hand upon the African Church and Africa's growing young population as God's new agent to drive the pro-life agenda of God. The Church can win, and will win, the abortion debate. All African Christians must read this book.

Rev. David GB Kiamu
President, Life Bible Missions College and Seminary

My pro-life ministry leadership journey started twenty-six years ago when I launched a crisis pregnancy center called Silent Voices in Zambia. God eventually allowed me to establish the Association for Life of Africa. *The African Awakening* explains a biblical culture of life, which I would recommend to our fellow African Churches and leaders. Many of our Church leaders have not fully understood God's heart about human life, and this book can be a valuable resource for Church leaders who desire to champion life and offer life ministries in the context of their local churches. I highly recommend this needed resource.

Barbra Mwansa
President, Association for Life of Africa

I will surely bless you, and I will surely multiply your offspring as the stars of heaven and as the sand that is on the seashore. And your offspring shall possess the gate of his enemies, and in your offspring shall all the nations of the earth be blessed, because you have obeyed my voice.
(Genesis 22:17-18, ESV)

THE AFRICAN AWAKENING

Bringing the Message of Life to the World

Raúl Reyes

bookVillages

The African Awakening: Bringing the Message of Life to the World
© 2024 Raúl Reyes

All rights reserved. No part of this publication may be reproduced in any form without written permission from Book Villages, P.O. Box 64526, Colorado Springs, CO 80962. www.bookvillages.com

Cover Design by Kurt Valenta, Art Director, Choose Life Marketing
Front and Back photos: 2004 Adobe Stock
Interior Design by Niddy Griddy Design, Inc.
Photo of Author: Krista Steed-Reyes
Graphic image of tree: iStock

Unless otherwise identified, all Scripture quotations in this publication are taken from the Holy Bible, New International Version® (NIV®). Copyright © 1973, 1978, 1984 by International Bible Society. Used by permission of Zondervan. All rights reserved. Other versions include: The Holy Bible, English Standard Version. ESV® Text Edition: 2016. Copyright © 2001 by Crossway Bibles, a publishing ministry of Good News Publishers; *Holy Bible*, New Living Translation, (NLT) copyright © 1996, 2004, 2015 by Tyndale House Foundation. Used by permission of Tyndale House Publishers, Inc., Carol Stream, Illinois 60188. All rights reserved; God's Word (GW) Copyright © 1995, 2003, 2013, 2014, 2019, 2020 by God's Word to the Nations Mission Society. All rights reserved; the New King James Version®. (NKJV) Copyright © 1982 by Thomas Nelson. Used by permission; King James Version (KJV), Public Domain. All rights reserved; New American Standard Bible®, (NASB) Copyright © 1960, 1971, 1977, 1995, 2020 by The Lockman Foundation. All rights reserved; International Standard Version (ISV), Copyright © 1995-2014 by ISV Foundation. ALL RIGHTS RESERVED INTERNATIONALLY. Used by permission of Davidson Press, LLC; NET Bible® copyright ©1996-2017 by Biblical Studies Press, L.L.C. http://netbible.com All rights reserved. SAINT JOSEPH NEW CATHOLIC BIBLE® Copyright © 2019 by Catholic Book Publishing Corp. Used with permission. All rights reserved.

ISBN: 978-1-95756-624-5
LCCN: 2024911599

Printed in the United States of America
1 2 3 4 5 6 7 8 / 28 27 26 25 24

To my beloved wife, Christine

With gratitude and love I dedicate this book to my wife, Christine. For forty-three years, you have been my faithful companion, my rock, and my partner in sharing the transformative message of Christ and life. Together, we have embarked on countless journeys, leading local, national, and international ministries, while touching the lives of countless individuals along the way. Your unwavering support, faith, and love have been my constant source of inspiration and encouragement.

You have helped me grow into the man of God I am today. Your wisdom, strength, and practical know-how have been indispensable in every ministry we have co-led. Through it all, your presence has been my sanctuary and solace. Whenever I am with you, I am home.

I am forever grateful for your partnership, dedication, and unwavering commitment to our shared mission. Without you, I cannot imagine where I would be. Christ has been the foundation upon which our journey has flourished, and I am eternally blessed to have had you by my side.

This book, a testament to our shared purpose and devotion (and your encouragement to "write that book!"), is a tribute to the extraordinary woman you are. May it serve as a reflection of the love, faith, and unwavering commitment that binds us together.

Table of Contents

Foreword	11
Acknowledgments	13
Preface	15
1. The Global Abortion Genocide	19
2. Crossroad of Death: The Intersection Between Africa and Abortion	35
3. Vanishing World: The Global Population Crisis	49
4. Africa's Prophetic Mandate: Delivering Christ's Message of Life to the World	61
5. Marriage: The Covenant for Life	77
6. Be Fruitful: The Divine Call to Multiply	103
7. Choices and Consequences: The Hidden Realities of Abortion Methods	117
8. Guardians of Life: Global Life-Affirming Ministries	141
About the Author	161
Get In Touch	163
Endnotes	165

Foreword

"The thief comes only to steal and kill and destroy; I have come that they may have life, and have it to the full" (John 10:10). This verse has been a defining statement of Jesus in my life. We find the cosmic battle between the Evil One, who is intent on taking life, and a Good Shepherd who comes to give life to the fullest.

That battle is playing out every day on the continent of Africa. On one hand, there is a growing and vibrant Church as the center of Christianity shifts from the West to the global South and East. Christianity took root in Africa soon after the death and resurrection of Christ and played a significant role in its spread. In recent years, Christianity has again been on the rise on the African continent.

At the same time, Africa has been a place where the diminishment of life has been a regular feature fueled by poverty, war, corruption, and the global holocaust of abortion, where millions of babies never see the light of day. The news is that the African Church is waking up to the call to become life-givers and champions of a culture of life rather than allowing the Thief to kill, steal, and destroy.

This *African Awakening* by my dear friend Raúl Reyes provides a needed road map for the African Church as to how the local church can champion life on behalf of the Good Shepherd and push back the tide of evil that the Thief wants to bring. In this book, you will find the tactics of the Evil One and their long-term ramifications. You will also find the Good News of Jesus and realize that every Christian and every local church can represent Him in preserving life and protecting the unborn.

I have spent many years observing the African Church, and this is what I know. When awakened, the African Church is an amazing and powerful force for Christ in society. It knows how to do much with little and understands God's power to do what we think is impossible.

That faith and action paradigm, fueled by God's Spirit and His truth, is why I am optimistic about the African Church and its response to this critical message of life.

I pray that each person who reads this book will answer the call to be an agent of life and push back the darkness of the Evil One. And I pray that every local church will become a place where life is celebrated and preserved, those who find themselves with unwanted pregnancies are ministered to, and unborn babies are saved.

I hope you will join the African Awakening and the Good Shepherd in bringing life and life to the full. Thank you, Raúl, for challenging the African Church as you do the global Church to the message of life, redemption, and healing.

TJ Addington
The Addington Method
Author, Consultant, and International Trainer

Acknowledgments

I would like to acknowledge the many people the Lord has used in my life to make this book a reality.

- Family
    - My mother Ligia Elba Reyes, who showed me how to love Jesus
    - My wife Christine Reyes, who teaches me every day
    - My children David Reyes, Stephen Reyes, Christina Schubert, Alaina Sankey, and Michael Reyes, who taught me what it means to be a pro-life father
    - My brothers, and especially Reiko, my best friend

- Mentors
    - Dick and Sandy Urie, who first called us into service
    - Christine and Larry Smith, who showed us how to serve
    - Tom and Lee Chapman, who taught me how to serve
    - David Everitt, who modeled how to serve
    - Phil White, who served alongside me
    - Tim Addington, who encourages me to continue serving

- Fellow Pro-Life Leaders
    - Anderson Ocampo
    - Bill and Debi Velker
    - Bramuel Musya
    - Brandon Monahan
    - Christine Reyes
    - Dinah Monahan
    - Don Parks
    - Ed and Jane Harrold
    - Edward and Barbra Mwansa
    - Evelyn Stone
    - Gail Friedman Barrett
    - Jeanne Pernia

- John Ensor
- Jor-El Godsey
- Kurt Dillinger
- Mark Nicholson
- Melissa Heiland
- Nelly and Michael Roach
- Pat Layton
- Peggy Hartshorn
- Roland Warren
- Simon and Johanna

- Life Equip Global Team
  - Christine Reyes
  - Dennis Rogers
  - Don Marshall
  - Ed Harrold
  - Marcie Little
  - Jeff and Nancy Anderson
  - Chris and Cyndi Carlson
  - Drs. Gary and Beth Jewell
  - Thomas Lothamer
  - Sharon Parks
  - Robert Foust

- Life Equip Global Financial Partners
- Pinnacle Forum Brothers
- Choose Life Marketing Family

And a special thanks to Richard and Sherri Hampton, who God used to help start Life Equip Global, and Michael and Nelly Roach, leaders of Choose Life Marketing—the largest pro-life marketing company in the world—that God is using to help take Life Equip Global to the global Church and to create a Global Life Coalition.

Preface

The year was 1982. I was twenty-six years old, and my wife, Christine, and I were pregnant with the first of five children. I was managing a Christian bookstore named Zondervan Family Bookstore. It was there that I read Francis Schaeffer's book *Whatever Happened to the Human Race?* That book changed our lives and led us into ministry leadership in the mission field created by abortion for the next forty-one years. That book was the spark that started a revolution in the way evangelical Christians thought about life and death, and its impact echoes down to today.

Whatever Happened to the Human Race? explained what the Bible says about the sanctity of human life and how the world had turned its back on life and had embraced the murder of babies through abortion. I felt like a spear was thrust into my heart as I read the book. How could I call myself a Christian, a spiritual warrior, a man of God, while thousands of babies just like mine growing in my wife's womb were being destroyed by abortion? My wife and I were totally convicted by what we read. We learned that a baby in the womb is a person and our neighbor.

We asked God to forgive us for how we had turned our backs on babies made in His image, and to use us in any way He saw fit to help save the lives of innocent babies. Not long after, we were invited to join the steering committee for a ministry that we would end up leading called the Pregnancy Center of Pinellas County. That was the beginning of what—so far—has been forty-one years of serving in the mission field created by abortion.

My prayer is that this book will impact you as powerfully as Dr. Schaeffer's book impacted my wife and me—as well as thousands of other Christian leaders. *The African Awakening* is really two books in one. In the first section you will see how Africa is under attack and learn how foreign governments and organizations are infiltrating Africa and spreading their poisonous lies while multiplying a culture of death. You will read about how the continent of Africa—that once experienced a diaspora of its people being forcibly ripped from the land, enslaved, and taken into countries around the world—will someday be the same continent that will bring a message of life to the world. This will happen when *negative population growth* starts devastating close to one hundred countries. At that time there will be a second diaspora, but one in which Africans will be bringing life to the world—through the sharing of the Gospel of Christ and the message of life—rather than the world taking the life out of Africa.

The second section is a basic handbook on some of life's most core issues including the value of human life, the importance of marriage, the role of sex, and God's design for the family. It will teach you what an abortion is and how an abortion kills children and damages men and women, as well as entire countries. It will also provide practical suggestions on what ministries you might consider starting to help multiply the message of life in Africa.

The enemy of life, Satan, has tried to minimize, marginalize, and ridicule the sanctity of the human life message. As a result, Christian leaders are either not aware of what the Bible says about the sanctity of human life or refuse to speak to the sanctity of life from the pulpit because:

- They are unaware of the killing of babies that is occurring in their countries.
- Their personal sin in this area keeps them from speaking out.
- They don't wish to offend anyone.
- They are afraid of losing church members.
- They don't understand that abortion is murder.
- They believe abortion is a political issue.
- They don't think abortion has anything to do with the Gospel.

- They are unaware of how many people in their church have been wounded by abortion.

The African Awakening will be extremely helpful to global leaders, movement leaders, bishops, pastors, Church leaders, and individuals who wish to understand and join God's work as we see end time prophecies being fulfilled before our eyes. *The African Awakening* is an exploration of abortion as well as the issues surrounding abortion including its impact on men and women, the rise of the Church in Africa, declining populations, and the impact the African Church will have on the world.

The world is not prepared for the global crash in the number of babies being born, which is set to have a cataclysmic impact on societies. Falling birth rates mean over one hundred countries could have shrinking populations by the end of the century. And twenty-three nations are expected to see their populations cut in half by 2100. Countries will also age dramatically, with as many people turning eighty as there are being born.[1] This book explains what these grim statistics will mean for the people of Africa.

As a result of my forty-plus years of ministry leadership and visits to thirty-three countries, I have found the following to be true:

1. Christians around the world are not knowledgeable about what the Bible has to say about the sanctity of human life.
2. Christians around the world are hungry to learn what the Bible has to say about the sanctity of human life.
3. Christians around the world apply what they have learned and make an immediate impact.

Christians have one mission—"Go and make disciples of all nations" (Matthew 28:19). The Samaritan woman at the well did just that. When she realized Jesus was the Messiah, she went back to her town and told everyone, "Come, see a man who told me everything I ever did" (John 4:29). Come and see. That is the good news we share with others. This book will equip Christians all over Africa so they can tell young women (and men) who feel hopeless, lost, and confused *come and see*.

> "Come and see that there is hope."
> "Come and see that your baby is a person."
> "Come and see that you are not alone."
> "Come and see that Jesus is the answer."
> "Come and see the plans God has for Africa!"

After reading this book, may your heart catch fire as mine did to share Christ's message of hope and life with those considering ending the life of their baby through abortion. May you be messengers of life, spreading His Good News throughout your church, your community, your country, throughout the continent of Africa, and throughout the world!

Chapter 1:
The Global Abortion Genocide

Around 2012 I had just completed a week of training on the sanctity of human life in a francophone country in Africa for about 200 local pastors. The training had deeply impacted everyone in attendance. On the last day we had a period of repentance and prayer. An older gentleman in the front row, wearing the most resplendent and beautiful yellow suit I had ever seen, stood up to talk. He was a well-respected national Christian pastor. The room immediately hushed. In French, and through our translator, he told the most unforgettable story. He said "You all know me from my over twenty years of Church leadership. What you don't know is that over twenty years ago I was a doctor. As a matter of fact, I was an abortionist." The room grew so quiet you could hear a pin drop.

"One late night as I was trying to sleep, I heard the sound of a newborn baby crying very near to my home, so I went outside to see why an irresponsible mother was letting a baby cry so near my house. When I went outside, the crying stopped—I heard nothing. Three times this happened, and each time I stepped outside only to hear silence. I finally fell asleep. Then I had a dream . . . or a vision. I started seeing the faces of babies. One after another. And somehow I knew they were the faces of the more than 300 babies I had killed by abortion. The next morning I knew God had allowed me to hear

> *the sounds of the babies that I had killed crying and allowed me to see their faces. I got up that morning, went to my clinic, locked it up, and never returned. Since that day I have dedicated myself to serving the Lord."*
>
> *That pastor had killed hundreds of children by abortion. But the Lord called him to repent and follow Him. This is a powerful story of the depth of God's love for us. This pastor—a former abortionist—has now helped countless lives come to Christ. He is healed, forgiven, and set free. I pray as you read this book that you too will have a personal encounter with Jesus and that whatever has occurred in your past, you will join us in embracing the call to share the Gospel of Christ and the Gospel of Life.*
>
> *Listening to that story changed the lives of over 200 pastors, including mine. Since then I have started an international ministry called Life Equip Global to equip the Church with sanctity of human life training.*
>
>
>
> *Raúl Reyes*
> *President*
> *Life Equip Global*
>
>

The killing of millions of babies around the world created in the image of God can only be described as a Global Abortion Genocide. This Global Abortion Genocide is Satan's plan for death and destruction of innocent preborn human beings on a global scale and an assault on those created in the image of God. This unprecedented and satanic Global Abortion Genocide demands an unprecedented response from the Church of Jesus Christ. We must understand that there is one entity behind the global destruction of babies. It's not governments, courts, medical systems, or the educational system that is behind the mass destruction of babies—it is Satan. He is the architect of death.

According to the Alan Guttmacher Institute, the annual number of abortions in Africa nearly doubled between 1995 to 1999 and 2015 to 2019, from 4.3 million to 8.0 million. With tens of millions of babies killed every year in the Global Abortion Genocide, and with millions of babies killed by abortion every year in Africa, there is much work to be done.[1] What kind of work? The work of equipping the Church. And why must we equip the Church? Because it is through the Church that the message of Life will be spread throughout the world. But first the Church must deal with some sad truths. Let's start with the sad truth that all over the world Christians, even pastors, are sending their wives, their daughters, and their congregations to have abortions. Why? Is it because they are evil? No. It is because they have not been taught the truth about babies made in the image of God, babies that are fully human, and babies that we are called to defend. They lack knowledge.

The Bible says, "My people are destroyed because they lack knowledge" (Hosea 4:6). The opposite is also true; people flourish when they gain knowledge. This book is written with the goal of providing you with the knowledge necessary to fight the Global Abortion Genocide.

Why do we even talk about abortion? Aren't there other issues we should be concerned with? Issues like war, hunger, homelessness, and disease? Yes, all of these issues should cause us great concern and need to be addressed. But abortion stands apart from all these issues.

An estimated total of seventy to eighty million people perished in World War II.[2] To compare, there are roughly seventy-three million abortions per year.[3] This brings us to the conclusion that abortion is the greatest destroyer of innocent human life ever seen in world history.

Preborn children represent the most persecuted, least protected, and most murdered group of people on the face of the Earth. In addition to the horror of killing babies in the womb every year, millions of men and women experience abortion's devastating physical damage and emotional pain. Abortion takes a baby's life and damages a woman's heart. When a pregnant woman enters an abortion clinic, two people enter, but only one comes out. The mother leaves behind the broken pieces of her baby but takes with her the broken pieces of her heart.

When the life of a preborn baby is ended, we are also ending the lives of the children, grandchildren, and great-grandchildren that baby would have had. When you end the life of one preborn child, you are ending the life of generations.

But thankfully, the opposite is also true. When you save the life of one preborn baby, you are saving the lives of all the children, grandchildren, and great-grandchildren of that child. That one child will become a mother or father who will have children. That one child will create future teachers, pastors, doctors, or engineers. People live and lives flourish.

Abortion not only ends the life of a child, but it also violates the fundamental role of a man as protector and strips a woman of her position as life-bearer. And ultimately it is an attack against God. Satan cannot attack the Creator, so he attacks God's greatest creation—His people. As Pastor John MacArthur stated, "Abortion is Satan's greatest onslaught against the sovereignty of God."[4] I believe abortion is the last official stand of the defiant apostate against God.

How should we respond against the Global Abortion Genocide? Proverbs 24:11-12 tells us: "Rescue those being led away to death; hold back those staggering toward slaughter. If you say, 'But we knew nothing about this,' does not he who weighs the heart perceive it? Does not he who guards your life know it? Will he not repay everyone according to what they have done?" This is a command from God, and He will not give us a command without giving us the ability to complete that command.

The Sin of Abortion

Abortion has affected hundreds of millions of lives, including many Christians—like the doctor in the beginning of this chapter. It is possible that you may have been impacted by abortion personally. Perhaps you know someone in your family who has had an abortion, or perhaps you encouraged someone you know and love to have an abortion, or perhaps you yourself have had an abortion. The information in this book is not meant to cause you pain or guilt or shame. Quite the opposite. This information is to remind us that there are consequences to our actions and of the incredible price that was paid at the cross by Jesus on our behalf—and the incredible gift that Christ's death on the cross provides us.

Abortion—the killing of an innocent baby in its mother's womb—is a grave sin against God. And every one of our sins is nailed to the cross. The Lord Jesus paid a price for us so that we might not suffer eternal separation from God, but be reconciled to the Father. This is the Gospel. The Good News. The blood of the cross covers every sin, including the sin of abortion. All we must do is believe. We are here to proclaim the Good News that Jesus—at the cross—broke every chain!

This book will prepare you to respond with hope, education, and the love of Christ to someone considering an abortion. It will equip you to share a message of hope and life with your church. It will start you on a journey to be an Ambassador of Life to your country and the countries around the world. Our goal is to see hearts renewed, healed, and transformed. This will only happen as the Church takes her rightful place as the sharer of love, hope, and truth. In order for this to occur, the Church needs teachers. This book can start you on a journey of becoming a life-giver–a person that is equipped to respond to a life-and-death situation with words of life. This book will equip you to save lives!

As a result you will join other Christians around the world who have taken the Lord's greatest commandment to heart. "'Teacher, which is the greatest commandment in the Law?' Jesus replied: "'Love the Lord your God with all your heart and with all your soul and with all your mind." This is the first and greatest commandment. And the second is like it: "Love your neighbor as yourself"'" (Matthew 22:36-39). And the knowledge we learn from this book is that babies in the womb are also our neighbors.

The Sanctity of Human Life

Embracing the sanctity of human life is not just a duty; it is our divine responsibility as followers of God. In recognizing the value placed upon each soul, we become stewards of His precious creation, advocates for the vulnerable, and instruments of His love. The sanctity of human life is why we defend children in the womb.

The right to life and the sanctity of human life, along with the urgency to protect and defend life, do not come from the government, courts, or any person's opinion. They come from God Himself. Because people are made in the image of God—and belong to God—it is a horrible crime against Him to kill an innocent person, to spill innocent blood. It is a crime against God! Whether the person is healthy or sick, rich or poor, young or old, in the womb or out of the womb, black, yellow, brown, red, or white—it doesn't matter. All people at every stage of development are made in the image of God. Two things are true of every person that exists now, that has ever existed, or that will exist in the future.

1. There goes one made in the image of God.
2. And there goes one for whom Christ died.

The sanctity of human life is defined as:

The reverence for and sacredness of each and every human life created in the image of God; based upon its intrinsic worth and equal value, regardless of its stage or condition, from conception until natural death.[5]

The Bible does not differentiate between human life in the womb or out of the womb. It sees them both as made in the image of God. In the Bible, both the Hebrew word *yeled* and the Greek word *brephos* are commonly used to refer to a baby either yet to be born or a newborn. In Genesis 25:22, the word *yeled* is used to describe Jacob and Esau struggling in their mother's womb. In Exodus 2:6, *yeled* is used to describe Moses as a baby in a basket. Similarly, in Luke 1:41, the Greek word *brephos* is used to refer to John the Baptist leaping in his mother Elizabeth's womb. In Luke 2:12 it is used to describe Jesus who was lying in the manger.

In the Word of God, God claims authorship over our creation.

> See now that I myself am he! There is no god besides me. I put to death and I bring to life, I have wounded and I will heal, and no one can deliver out of my hand. (Deuteronomy 32:39)

> The LORD brings death and makes alive; he brings down to the grave and raises up. (1 Samuel 2:6)

> For you created my inmost being; you knit me together in my mother's womb. (Psalm 139:13)

> Before I formed you in the womb I knew you, before you were born I set you apart. (Jeremiah 1:5)

While the Bible speaks clearly about God's sovereignty over all of His creation, it makes a special distinction for mankind—men and women—for we are the *only* beings created in the image of God.

So God created mankind in his own image, in the image of God he created them; male and female he created them. (Genesis 1:27)

For Christians, it is the fact that every person, believer or unbeliever, either unborn or newborn, is created *in the image of God* that gives people substance, honor, and the very need to preserve and protect life. This distinction is not reserved only for the followers of Christ, but extends to every member of the human race from the first instant of conception until our last natural breath.

Finally God commands us not to kill. In Exodus 20:13 God states clearly and distinctly: "You shall not murder." The command refers to taking innocent life. Abortion is the intentional taking of the life of an innocent child, made in the image of God, while still in its mother's womb.

These biblical truths compel us to speak of the sanctity of all human life and against the satanic Global Abortion Genocide. By embracing and teaching this truth to others, we can tear down Satan's strongholds of ignorance and lies, and equip the Church with the powerful truth that *all people*, starting at conception, are made in the image of God and deserve to be protected.

Jesus died for all of us! Every life—starting at the very first instant of conception—is to be valued and held as sacred, because every person is made in the very image of God. With the power of God, we stand against the Global Abortion Genocide and literally save lives.

Abortion Statistics

The Alan Guttmacher Institute and the World Health Organization place global abortions at seventy-three million a year. More than half of unintended pregnancies (61 percent) end in abortion.[6] According to the World Health Organization, abortion is allowed in some form in approximately 125 out of 195 countries. In many countries, babies in the womb are not protected by law and can be killed for little or no reason at all. In every country, preborn babies are being killed either through surgical, chemical, or traditional abortion means, including infanticide, or killing the baby immediately after it is born.

Over sixty-three million abortions have occurred in the United States alone since 1973.[7] It is estimated that India has over fifteen million babies killed by abortion,[8] and China has thirteen million surgical abortions and over ten million abortion pills sold.[9] In India, nearly eight women die from causes related to abortions every day.[10] The continent of Asia has the largest number of abortions in the world. In addition, ninety-six countries have approved the baby-killing drug Mifepristone.[11]

Abortion in Africa

According to the Alan Guttmacher Institute, during 2010 to 2014, an estimated 8.2 million induced abortions occurred each year in Africa. The proportion of pregnancies ended by abortion range from 12 percent in Western Africa to 24 percent in Southern Africa.[12] Since 2019, Sub-Saharan Africa has the highest rate of abortion-related deaths in the world, at 15,000, which means that there are 185 maternal deaths per 100,000 abortions.[13] Abortion is legal to some degree in forty-four out of the fifty-four countries in Africa.[14]

Satan and Child Sacrifice

Satan is a fallen angel and the enemy and adversary of human life. Since God created man, Satan has waged war against humanity. He is the architect of all the evil we see in the world today, including the Global Abortion Genocide. Satan has been in the business of people killing people, starting with innocent babies before and after birth, from the beginning of history. God wants us to understand and overcome our enemy. To do that, we must recognize Satan's strategies and know God's countermeasures. We need to know what His weapons are. We need to be aware, but not afraid.

> For our struggle is not against flesh and blood, but against the rulers, against the authorities, against the powers of this dark world and against the spiritual forces of evil in the heavenly realms. Therefore put on the full armor of God, so that when the day of evil comes, you may be able to stand your ground, and after you have done everything, to stand. (Ephesians 6:12-13)

> He [the devil] was a murderer from the beginning, not holding to the truth, for there is no truth in him. When he lies, he speaks his native language, for he is a liar and the father of lies. (John 8:44)

We also read that "Cain who was of the wicked one" (the devil) (1 John 3:12, NKJV). So Satan incited the first murder recorded in history when Cain killed his brother Abel.

The connection between Pharaoh ordering the killing of Jewish baby boys in Exodus 1:15-22 and Herod ordering the killing of babies two years and younger in Matthew 2:16-18 can be seen as a form of satanic attack. In both cases, the attacks were designed to prevent the Jewish people from fulfilling their God-given destiny and purpose. Satan was trying to prevent the Deliverer from being born and the Messiah from coming into the world. The fact that Moses the Deliverer, and Jesus the Messiah, were both able to come into the world despite these attacks is a testament to God's power and protection.

In Deuteronomy 12:31 we learn about babies that were offered as sacrifices to idols. "You must not worship the LORD your God in their way, because in worshiping their gods, they do all kinds of detestable things the LORD hates. They even burn their sons and daughters in the fire as sacrifices to their gods."

"You shall not give any of your children to offer them to Molech, and so profane the name of your God: I am the LORD" (Leviticus 18:21, ESV). Those who worshiped Molech often sacrificed their own children, who were ritually murdered and then placed on the sacrificial altar of fire. Abortion kills a baby before he or she is ready to be born; child sacrifice kills a child who is already born. Both are the sacrifice of a child's life. The only difference between abortion and child sacrifice is the age of the baby and the location where the baby is killed.

In addition, the Bible tells us that the taking of innocent blood pollutes the land. "You shall not pollute the land in which you live, for [innocent] blood pollutes the land, and no atonement can be made for the land for the blood that is shed in it, except by the blood of the one who shed it" (Numbers 35:33, ESV). The blood of the innocent also cries out to God. "And the LORD said, 'What have you done? The voice of your brother's blood is crying to me from the ground'" (Genesis 4:10, ESV).

Satan is still in the business of encouraging us to offer up the lives of our children through the sacrifice of abortion. And he is still the father of lies. Lies like:

- Abortion is your right.
- It's your body; it's your choice.
- It's not really a baby.
- Abortion is reproductive health.

Satan hates us because we bear the image of God, but he has no power over believers that are filled with the Holy Spirit. He does, however, have plenty of power and influence over lost people in this fallen world, and that power can be used in ways that can negatively impact our lives including imprisoning, torturing, and even killing Christians and babies.

We fight against spiritual forces, but God has given us spiritual power. Our defense is the Word of God, worship, and prayer.

For though we live in the world, we do not wage war as the world does. The weapons we fight with are not the weapons of the world. On the contrary, they have divine power to demolish strongholds. We demolish arguments and every pretension that sets itself up against the knowledge of God, and we take captive every thought to make it obedient to Christ. (2 Corinthians 10:3-5)

But the Lord is faithful and he will strengthen you and protect you from the evil one. (2 Thessalonians 3:3)

No, in all these things we are more than conquerors through him who loved us. For I am convinced that neither death nor life, neither angels nor demons, neither the present nor the future, nor any powers, neither height nor depth, nor anything else in all creation, will be able to separate us from the love of God that is in Christ Jesus our Lord. (Romans 8:37-39)

Be strong in the Lord and in his mighty power. Put on the full armor of God, so that you can take your stand against the devil's schemes. (Ephesians 6:10-11)

The Abortion Giant

Abortion and those who support abortion seem to be unstoppable. They have billions of dollars at their disposal and a network that spans the globe. In the U.S. the average cost for a first trimester abortion is about $500. If we assume that the cost globally for an abortion is even half that much, that still means the abortion industry is raking in over $18 billion annually. That doesn't include the huge amounts they receive from government grants. Many governments, educational institutions, private foundations, and medical organizations are promoting abortion. Large, private pro-abortion corporations exist solely to promote abortion and birth control. When you add it all up, abortion seems like an unbeatable foe.

The Bible tells us a story of another seemingly unbeatable foe. David was a teenage boy when he went to bring food to his brothers who were with the army of Israel. They were being taunted and terrified by Goliath who was 2.7 meters (nine feet) tall. Goliath seemed unbeatable. His armor alone weighed fifty-seven kilograms (125 pounds). His spear was over 3.6 meters long (twelve feet long) and weighed over fifteen kilograms (thirty-three pounds). But David was not afraid. He had already killed a bear and a lion using a sling. He knew it was God who destroys the enemy. He just needed to be obedient.

David had righteous anger. "Who is this uncircumcised Philistine that he should defy the armies of the living God?" he said in 1 Samuel 17:26. Yes, David knew that with God on his side, even the seemingly unbeatable Goliath could be killed. But David needed one thing: *ammunition*. So he went and found five smooth stones. With this book, the Lord is equipping us with ammunition—our very own five smooth stones—to defeat the giant of abortion.

Five Smooth Stones

1. Love—Demonstrate the love of God by showing love, mercy, and compassion.
2. Truth—Help people understand the truth that the baby is alive, and that abortion is the killing of an innocent baby. Tell them about God and Jesus.
3. Knowledge—Educate mothers about how abortions are done and how an abortion will kill her baby and potentially harm her emotionally, physically, and spiritually.

4. Hope—Help people understand that they are not alone. That God has sent *you* to help.
5. Courage—Provide courage by encouraging those who are discouraged.

Like David, we should have true righteous anger at Satan's Global Abortion Genocide which is the killing of millions of innocent babies, made in the image of God, every year. David had courage and a cause. He stood against and defeated a giant. So can we! Because the battle is the Lord's! The Bible tells us to "fear not" 365 times. With the Lord on our side, there is *no enemy* that can stand against us. Romans 8:31 states, "If God is for us, who can be against us?"

What It Means to Be Pro-Life

Most people think being pro-life means standing against abortion. But it means so much more. Being pro-life means being *for the sanctity of every human life from conception to natural death*. It means recognizing that every person is created in the image of God and has inherent worth and dignity, and therefore deserves to be protected and defended. As Christians, we are called to value the sanctity of all human life. This includes the vulnerable and marginalized members of society, such as the elderly, the disabled, the homeless, and the poor. It includes those who have mistreated us, or hurt us, who disagree with us, or who we see as an enemy. It especially includes how we treat our spouse and children. Christians who are pro-life believe in the importance of promoting a culture of life, where *every* person is valued and protected.

The Bible emphasizes the importance of caring for the hungry, homeless, those in prison, and the enslaved. Here are a few examples.

> Is not this the kind of fasting I have chosen: to loose the chains of injustice and untie the cords of the yoke, to set the oppressed free and break every yoke? Is it not to share your

food with the hungry and to provide the poor wanderer with shelter—when you see the naked, to clothe them, and not to turn away from your own flesh and blood? (Isaiah 58:6-7)

For I was hungry and you gave me food, I was thirsty and you gave me drink, I was a stranger and you welcomed me, I was naked and you clothed me, I was sick and you visited me, I was in prison and you came to me. (Matthew 25:35-36, ESV)

Open your mouth for the mute, for the rights of all who are destitute. Open your mouth, judge righteously, defend the rights of the poor and needy. (Proverbs 31:8-9, ESV)

Ultimately, being pro-life means recognizing the inherent value and dignity of *every* human being, and working to uphold and defend this value in all its forms. It means caring for the preborn, the homeless, the hungry, and all those who are vulnerable or marginalized. As Christians, we have a responsibility to love and serve our neighbors, and to work toward a world where every person is treated with dignity, respect, and compassion.

Being willing to help needy people is a key part of being pro-life. But we can't really say we are pro-life if we aren't willing to start by helping the most persecuted, least protected, most often killed people group on Earth—babies in the womb.

The Good News

The unprecedented satanic Global Abortion Genocide demands an unprecedented response from the Church of Jesus Christ. The information found in this book is part of that response. When we use the anointing of the Holy Spirit, the armor of God, the power found in the Word of God, and the knowledge shared in this book, we can help free those who have been enslaved by Satan's lies. And you can help save lives! We are to be like Jesus who said, "The thief comes only to steal and kill and destroy. I came that they may have life and have it abundantly" (John 10:10, ESV). The gates of hell cannot prevail against the Church of Jesus Christ. "And I tell you, you are Peter, and on this rock I will build my church, and the gates of hell shall not prevail against it" (Matthew 16:18, ESV).

Conclusion

The multiplication of babies being killed by abortion around the world can only be called a Global Abortion Genocide. This mass scale killing of innocent babies is planned and led by Satan—the adversary of all human beings. God has provided us the weapons, and now we need to tear down the plans of the architect of death. Through embracing and sharing the powerful biblical truth about the sanctity of human life, the Church around the world, and especially in Africa, can stand against the greatest killing of innocent human beings in the history of mankind. You are more than a conqueror—your weapons are mighty for the tearing down of strongholds. The Lord Himself strengthens and protects you. Put on the full armor of the Lord and go forth victorious in battle!

Chapter 2:
Crossroad of Death: The Intersection Between Africa and Abortion

I was six years old when I woke up one day and found Mom was gone. Of four children I was the second born. Within three weeks, a nightmare started and everything changed. We had a new stepmother who came with two older children. Dad didn't share anything about where our mother was, and because we were in a shame culture, we couldn't ask what was going on.

Not long after, our stepmom started mistreating us—from not feeding us to not providing us with emotional support. We could not disclose the ill treatment to our father for fear that she would beat us to death. The abuse continued to an extent that we all started running away from home to seek refuge with relatives who were also not ready to receive us or to neighbors who could give us some meals.

My elder sister fell pregnant at fourteen years old and gave birth to a baby boy. During her pregnancy, she survived lots of abuse from my stepmother. After her child was able to walk, she became pregnant a second time. This time, she never told anyone because of the fear of abuse she got at first. She ran away to live with my auntie in the village and later drank an herb to abort her baby—but ended up dying. I was working and living in another city when I heard my sister had died.

While at boarding school, I fell in love with a teacher. I became pregnant by him, and even though he tried to stop me from aborting, with the experiences my sister went through and the fear of parents (since I was still in secondary school), I aborted. Later I fell pregnant again, and again I aborted. So I had two abortions. I still managed to finish school and went to college.

In 1994, I got married, and my husband had no idea of my past abortions. My husband felt the Lord calling him to serve Him. I encouraged him, and we both left for seminary. Between my husband and me, God blessed us with six pregnancies; unfortunately four children were stillborn, but two boys were saved. During the whole process of struggling to have children, there was a connection to a crisis pregnancy center in the United States called Silent Voices. I left for the U.S. to be part of a workshop to receive healing from the loss of my stillborn children. The abortions were still a huge secret in my life, and I didn't want my husband (who was now a pastor) to know about this.

At the session, women started sharing about their past abortions. Fear immediately crippled my heart! Three women before me shared about their past abortions, and I was the fourth one to share. When my time came, I felt I had no choice but to let out the secret. Immediately I felt something leave my body! I received my freedom! It was at that time that I strongly felt the Lord calling me to help women on the continent of Africa even though I didn't know how, because there was still the issue of my husband not knowing about my two abortions.

Back in Zambia, my heart was desiring to set up a pregnancy center, but I was still holding on to the fear of breaking the abortion news to my husband. Every time he wanted to talk about my training in the States, I would block him. But I was still feeling the need to launch out and do something for the girls in our country. One

> day, in April 1998, I broke the silence! I told my husband the truth! That truth set me free, and it helped me start the first crisis pregnancy center in Zambia called Silent Voices. The Lord also helped me start and lead the Association for Life of Africa (AFLA)—the largest pro-life ministry in Africa, which currently has over 300 pregnancy centers in twenty-three countries under our umbrella.
>
> The Lord has blessed me with two sons and one daughter—but I know that I have six children in heaven with the Lord!
>
> Barbra Mwansa
President and Founder
Association for Life of Africa (AFLA)

The Pro-Choice Agenda

In recent years there has been a growing pro-choice movement in Africa advocating for increased access to abortion.[1] The pro-choice agenda leaves behind many damaged men and women, like Barbra. It is extremely important to understand that those who champion abortion as a "right" have a much bigger agenda in mind. Let's be clear, those who call themselves pro-choice are championing the killing of babies through abortion. A better term is pro-abortion. And pro-abortion doesn't stop at promoting abortion. It includes promoting sexual reproductive rights, population control, sexual freedom, and LGBTQ+ acceptance.[2] From their perspective, multiplying the use of contraceptives and abortion represents hope and progress. This chapter addresses how this evil initiative is making inroads in Africa. To be forewarned is to be forearmed!

Africa is considered by many to be the birthplace of humanity.[3] This may be one of the reasons that Satan has a target on Africa. There is a concerted effort to multiply the evils of the West in Africa.

This includes drugs, sexual immorality, pornography, and abortion. Satan intends abortion to be a crossroad of death for Africa. What pro-choicers call Sexual Reproductive Rights is actually a euphemism for birth control and abortion.[4] One of the reasons pro-abortionists champion abortion is to decrease the population. There are significant similarities between eugenics and the pro-choice perspective on the need to limit population. Both ideologies share a focus on controlling and manipulating human life based on certain criteria or ideals. Like eugenics, the pro-choice position includes limiting population growth, often through the promotion of contraception, abortion, or sterilization, based on factors such as economic considerations or environmental impact.[5] Both approaches disregard the fundamental principle that all human beings have the right to exist and flourish regardless of their characteristics or circumstances.

Pro-abortionists and others who believe that the world is overpopulated believe that too many people are like a deadly virus.[6,7,8] The elimination of humans by whatever means—whether it be through abortion, sickness, war, or by the use of birth control—all help them achieve their goal: a world with less people. They also believe that promoting environmental sustainability by decreasing the population will preserve Africa's biodiversity for future generations.[9]

Sexual freedom is another value being promoted. They believe that encouraging sexual freedom involves challenging traditional values surrounding sexuality.[10] One of the ways they attack traditional values is by promoting comprehensive sex education, and what they call "non-judgmental attitudes." They encourage young boys and girls to question their sexuality and explore alternative sexual beliefs such as homosexuality, transgenderism, and all sexual expressions promoted by the LGBQT+ movement.[11] This fosters a sexually permissive and contagious atmosphere where the sin of sexual immorality multiplies. Make no mistake that their goal is to normalize the acceptance of the lesbian, gay, bisexual, queer, and transgender plus lifestyles—which means all manner of sexually immoral lifestyles.[12]

Remember that whenever you hear the terms *Reproductive Healthcare* or *Reproductive Rights* they are talking about abortion. How do pro-abortionists promote *Reproductive Rights,* in Africa? Those advancing acceptance of abortion on the continent of Africa have embraced a strategic approach that considers cultural sensitivities, legal frameworks, and public opinion.

Here is a list of strategic steps that are being taken to promote acceptance of abortion in Africa:

1. Advocacy and Awareness

a. Educate, in other words brainwash, the public. Conduct comprehensive awareness campaigns to disseminate misinformation about abortion, its legality, and the importance of reproductive rights.[13]

b. Engage with influential stakeholders. Pro-abortionists collaborate with religious leaders, community influencers, healthcare professionals, and policymakers to encourage them to embrace an abortion-positive philosophy. They do this by focusing on the importance of choice, women's health, and the so-called social and economic benefits of abortion. In other words, if we have less babies, we can have more material goods.

2. Legal Reforms and Policy Change

a. Review and reform existing laws. Pro-choicers conduct a thorough assessment of existing laws related to abortion in a country and, with support and funding from the West, advocate for legalizing the killing of babies through abortion. This includes making abortion legal, expanding the reasons why a woman can have an abortion, and multiplying the use of surgical and chemical abortions.[14]

b. Strengthen healthcare regulations. Develop guidelines and protocols for healthcare providers, teaching them how to do abortions up to a Western standard. By doing this they then say they are encouraging *safe* abortions.[15]

3. **Provide Access to Comprehensive Reproductive Healthcare**
   a. Under the guise of "improving healthcare infrastructure," pro-choicers bring Western money to invest in healthcare facilities, particularly in rural areas, to turn them into abortion clinics. This includes training healthcare providers, equipping facilities, and establishing referral networks to provide abortions.[16]
   b. Expand family planning services. Part of their plan is to increase access to contraceptives and family planning services, which they say is to prevent unintended pregnancies and reduce the need for abortion. However, the reality is that it often increases unplanned pregnancies and abortions.
   c. Increase comprehensive sex education in school like promoting sex before marriage, birth control, abortions, and counseling on birth control options.[17]

4. **Provide Counseling Services**
   a. They then seek to establish counseling services for individuals facing unplanned pregnancies, where they will strongly promote abortion as the only reasonable solution to an unplanned pregnancy. These so-called "counseling services" then funnel the unsuspecting girls to the local abortion clinic, for a fee of course.[18]
   b. Address socioeconomic barriers. The pro-abortion agenda wants people to believe they also address financial and social barriers that hinder access to abortion services, such as poverty, stigma, and lack of social support; again with Western dollars supporting social welfare programs and community initiatives. Unsuspecting African women are provided with everything they could possibly need to kill their babies by abortion.[19]

5. **Research and Data Collection**
   a. They conduct research on the impact of what they call *unsafe abortions* in order to promote *safe abortions*. In other words, surgical and chemical abortions.[20]

6. **International Support and Partnerships**
   a. Those in the pro-abortion movement are experts in acquiring international collaboration in support of advancing acceptance of abortion.[21]

The abortion movement never met an abortion it didn't like, except for what they term *unsafe abortions*, which are usually traditional abortions. But their solution is not seeking to eliminate abortion altogether; instead they are intent on promoting abortion techniques which they deem *safe*. But since an abortion always kills a living person, there is no such thing as a safe abortion.

The Church in Africa must be aware of this diabolic attack against the children, the families, the very core of Africa. And be prepared to respond with prayer, the Word of God, and a commitment to maintain, restore, and defend the sanctity of human life, traditional marriage, and biblical sexuality in Africa.

Africa and the Creation of Life

Many theologians and scholars have put forth arguments suggesting that the Garden of Eden—where God first created people—was located in Africa.[22] While the exact location remains uncertain, there are compelling reasons to consider Africa as a possible location for the biblical Garden. The first mention of the Garden of Eden is in Genesis. "The LORD God planted a garden eastward in Eden, and there He put the man whom He had formed" (Genesis 2:8, NKJV). Also, "Now a river went out of Eden to water the garden, and from there it parted and became four riverheads" (Genesis 2:10, NKJV). The Bible mentions four rivers flowing out of Eden: the Pishon, Gihon, Tigris, and Euphrates. Some scholars propose that the Pishon might be the Nile or one of its tributaries, while the Gihon could be the modern-day Nile, the Blue Nile, or the Atbara River—all of which are located in Africa.

The fact that God first created life in the Garden of Eden and the belief that the Garden of Eden was (or could have been) in Africa coincides with what science believes. Based on evidence from various fields, including genetics, anthropology, and archaeology, scientists believe that human life began in Africa. The most compelling evidence comes from studies of human DNA, which have revealed that all modern humans trace their ancestry back to a single population that lived in Africa. These findings, combined with the diversity of human genetic variation in African populations, suggest that the African continent was where God first created human beings in His image. The "Out of Africa" theory proposes that early humans migrated from Africa to populate the rest of the world, leading to the establishment of human populations in the rest of the world.[23]

Prior to European colonialism, it is estimated that Africa had up to 10,000 different states and independent groups with distinct languages and customs. Today, Africa has the youngest median age of populations in the world at around twenty years old. Unfortunately Africa also has the lowest life expectancy at around fifty-eight years. Africa is the second largest continent in the world with fifty-four countries—second only to Asia. Africa currently is home to over 3,000 ethnic groups who speak more than 2,000 languages. Africa today is a diverse continent with rich cultural heritage, vibrant economies, and a rapidly growing population of 1.35 billion. The United Nations' "World Population Prospects 2019" estimated that the population of Africa would increase from around 1.3 billion in 2020 to 4.2 billion by 2100.[24, 25]

Africa's Resources

It is a common belief that Africa is a poor continent. I would argue with that belief. Africa actually has the greatest resources of any continent on Earth.[26] Africa, often referred to as the "resource-rich continent," possesses an abundance of valuable minerals and other natural resources. The continent's diverse geology and vast landscapes have endowed it with an extensive array of resources, contributing to its significant potential for economic growth and development.

Africa's rich resources offer immense potential for economic development. But none of these are Africa's greatest resource. *Africa's greatest resource is its children!* Children that each come with incredible abilities, gifts, and blessings from God. Children who could transform the promise of Africa into reality. The people of Africa must awaken to the reality that Satan is targeting the children, the future of Africa. Indeed, he is targeting children all over the world with a Global Abortion Genocide.

The Western Myth of Overpopulation

For many years, Western governments and institutions have held the strong belief that the world is overpopulated. This myth has led to deadly consequences, especially for the nations of Africa.[27] For decades, the Western world has harbored concerns about global overpopulation, predicting dire consequences such as mass starvation, running out of drinking water, and the collapse of world systems. For years, due to the mistaken belief in overpopulation, Western governments and institutions have been exporting abortion and birth control measures to Africa in an attempt to limit population growth and decrease poverty. However, this mistaken and deadly approach fails to consider the unique context of rural African countries, where larger families can bring significant benefits. Embracing the advantages of larger families, such as increased labor for agriculture and social support systems, could have been a more appropriate solution.[28]

Far from having a problem with overpopulation, the truth is we are living in a far different reality, with numerous countries experiencing negative population growth. What is needed is a dependence on God and His Word as well as better resource management, rather than embracing a philosophy of death that relies solely on birth control and abortion.

The West Brings Abortion to Africa

In Africa, traditional cultural, religious, and legal norms have, up until recently, kept the killing of babies by abortion relatively low. In recent years, however, some African countries impacted by Western sexual values and pressured by Western governments led by the U.S. have begun to embrace Western sexual practices resulting in many more unwanted pregnancies and the liberalization of abortion laws. This has resulted in an explosive increase in the number of babies killed by abortions.

With the arrival of European colonizers, Western perspectives on abortion, influenced by secular ideologies, began to challenge traditional African values. This has greatly increased the number of abortions in Africa, which has contributed greatly to rising maternal mortality rates. The U.S. government, through foreign aid and policy, has played a role in shaping abortion practices in Africa.[29] Western population and research institutes, driven by secular ideologies, have advocated for the expansion of abortion in Africa. International organizations, such as the International Planned Parenthood Federation, are huge advocates for expanding abortion access in Africa.[30] Western pharmaceutical companies are also supplying abortion-inducing drugs and equipment throughout Africa.[31] Western influences, including the U.S. government, organizations, and international corporations, are contributing to the proliferation of abortion in Africa.

The U.S. government has played a significant role in promoting liberal attitudes regarding sexuality and reproductive health in Africa through the strategic use of grants and funding.[32] By providing financial support to governments in Africa, the U.S. has incentivized, or bribed, these governments to implement programs and initiatives that promote comprehensive sexual education, access to contraception, and reproductive health services—which means providing abortions.

Through targeted grants, the U.S. government has encouraged

African governments to adopt immoral sexual and reproductive health programs similar to those embraced by the West.³³ By linking funding to the promotion of liberal attitudes toward sexuality and reproductive health, the U.S. government has fostered partnerships with African governments that promote abortion and sexual immorality. This is a common strategy and approach used by the U.S. government and international organizations to promote liberal attitudes regarding sexuality and abortion in various regions, including Africa.

Abortion laws and their liberalization vary across African countries. In fourteen countries, including the Democratic Republic of the Congo, Senegal, South Sudan, and Egypt, abortion is completely illegal, while others permit it under certain circumstances such as saving the life of the mother or in cases of rape or fetal abnormalities.³⁴ These laws are seldom enforced, and therefore are not truly limiting the use of abortions. There has been a notable trend of increased liberalization of abortion laws in some African countries in recent years with forty-four countries allowing abortion to some degree. But even in countries in Africa where abortion is restricted, its practice is widespread with millions of babies being killed by abortion. According to the World Health Organization (WHO), an estimated 14 percent of all maternal deaths in Africa are due to abortions. This translates to thousands of women losing their lives each year as a result of abortion practices.³⁵

There now exist many well-financed international governments, corporations, businesses, and institutions who have targeted Africa for a multiplication of their values that include sexual confusion (LGBTQ+ philosophy), freedom of all types of sexual expression outside of marriage, mass distribution of contraceptives, and a focus on *Reproductive Healthcare* and *Reproductive Freedom*. This means supporting a multiplication of contraception and abortion or the killing of innocent babies. These organizations include:

U.S. Government-Based Entities
- USAID
- Office of Global Women's Issues
- Centers for Disease Control
- United States Global AIDS Coordinator
- United Nations Population Fund

Other Organizations
- Marie Stopes International Africa (Headquartered in England)
- Planned Parenthood International (Headquartered in the U.S.)
- African Women's Development Fund (Headquartered in Ghana)
- Pathfinder International (Headquartered in the U.S.)
- African Institute for Development Policy (Headquartered in Malawi)
- Center For Reproductive Rights (Headquartered in the U.S.)
- Women's Global Network for Reproductive Rights (Headquartered in the Philippines)
- African Population and Health Research Center (Headquartered in Kenya)
- International Planned Parenthood Federation (Headquartered in England)
- African Coalition for Maternal, Newborn, and Child Health
- Bill and Melinda Gates Foundation (Headquartered in the U.S.)

These organizations support *Reproductive Health*, which includes distribution of family planning aids (contraceptives) and promoting the use of abortion. For these organizations, progress is defined as more and more countries in Africa increasing access to contraceptives and eliminating any law that limits abortions. Examples of countries that have undergone significant legal changes regarding abortion include South Africa, Mozambique, and Tunisia.

The Church's Role in Africa

The Church in Africa has witnessed unprecedented growth in recent years. There are over 650 million Christians in Africa, more than on any other continent in the world, and it is the fastest-growing church in the world.[36] As of 2023, 96 percent of the population in Zambia, 95 percent of Seychelles, and 94 percent of the Rwanda population proclaim to be Christian. Africa is set to be the global center of Christianity for the next seventy-five years, or longer! This remarkable expansion is not only a testament to the power of faith, but also reflects the transformations taking place across the continent.

As the Church continues to expand, it has the potential to shape the social, cultural, and spiritual landscape of Africa—and the world—bringing hope, healing, and the message of Christ to hundreds of millions. The growing Church in Africa is the only institution that can respond to and defeat the Global Abortion Genocide occurring in Africa. Christians representing the body of Christ are the only ones capable of fighting the spiritual Goliath of abortion and defeating it, not with physical weapons, but through prayer and the Word of God, and by sharing truth, love, and knowledge.

We fight Global Abortion Genocide by teaching about the sanctity of human life and encouraging those who are pregnant to choose life for their babies. The Church alone has the ability to speak biblically about God's design for life and sex. The Church alone, teaching from the Bible, can encourage men and women to defend life and encourage people to tear down the idols of abortion and sex. But before the Church in Africa can become a beacon of life and love and hope to the nations in Africa and beyond, it needs to be equipped with solid biblical training on the sanctity of human life. That is why Life Equip Global exists. In chapter 8, you will read about our ministry and all the services and resources we provide.

The understanding that life begins at conception is deeply rooted in the Word of God as it aligns with the fact that every individual is created in the image of God. As a result, some Christian churches have spoken up to protect unborn babies and promote alternatives to abortion. This includes adoption and supporting pregnant mothers in difficult situations. There are a number of denominations, though, who have embraced abortion as a woman's right and who, to their great shame, even pay for women's abortions. Unfortunately the number of churches speaking out forcefully against the murder of preborn babies has been relatively few. In the future, our prayer is that an unwavering commitment to the sanctity of human life and a bold commitment to share this truth with others will make the Christian Church an important and influential voice in the ongoing debate surrounding abortion and the protection of human life at all stages. Pastors need to speak up and speak out regarding the killing of innocent babies!

Conclusion

We are seeing a powerful move of the enemy promoting abortion, liberal sexuality, and homosexual philosophies in the continent of Africa. As the Church in Africa continues to grow, it will have one of the most influential voices on the continent. That is why it is vital that we bring the teaching on the sanctity of human life to the Church in Africa. While Satan intends on bringing death to Africa by multiplying the killing of babies through abortion, God intends to use Africa to bring the message of life to the world.

African Christians representing the body of Christ are the only ones capable of fighting the spiritual Goliath of abortion and defeating it, not with physical weapons, but through prayer and the Word of God. Some pastors and Christians have made the argument that they can't talk about abortion because they are only called to share the Gospel. The truth is we never have to choose between sharing the Gospel and defending innocent preborn life. We must always do both!

Chapter 3:
Vanishing World: The Global Population Crisis

A number of years ago I was in Kenya sharing information about the sanctity of human life with about 200 or so Maasai pastors and their wives. As was the custom, the men sat on my right side and the women sat on the left. On the last day, after a full week of training, we reached a powerful time when we asked anyone who felt the need to confess and repent from past sins regarding abortion. The women almost immediately began praying, crying, and wailing. They had experienced unimaginable amounts of pain and emotional damage not only from abortion, but from rape, incest, and sexual abuse. This was the first time any of them had been allowed to express the pain they had been hiding. The crying out continued for quite some time, with the women sharing their pain and regret with their heavenly Father.

When the grief of the women subsided, it was the men's turn. The men then made a circle around the women and prayed over them, while confessing their own sins, which included not being there to protect the women. Many men openly confessed sins they had kept secret for many years. Secrets about abortion, and mistreating women, and bearing children out of marriage. There was a complete openness and feeling of repentance.

What happened next was truly amazing and an experience I

> will never forget. Rejoicing broke out. The Holy Spirit touched all these hearts, and they experienced God's forgiveness and healing. For the next few hours there was singing and dancing as I had never seen before. I witnessed with my own eyes the result of the Holy Spirit touching and healing wounded lives.
>
> This experience made clear to me that what Satan means for evil God means for good.
>
> Raúl Reyes
President
Life Equip Global

Negative Population Growth

In the previous chapter we discussed the negative impact of abortion on people, especially women. What about the impact of abortion on the world? While the world has experienced dynamic growth in population in the last 100 years, that time of population growth is coming to a crashing halt,[1] except on the continent of Africa. This chapter examines the factors causing negative population growth including abortion, infertility, birth control, and delayed marriage as well as the challenges it poses to economies and governments.

Data from the Population Reference Bureau show that currently there are twenty countries in the world with negative population growth—with some saying the number is closer to thirty.[2] That number will continue to grow every year and is expected to reach over ninety countries in negative population growth by 2100.[3] Negative growth of a population occurs when the overall number of individuals within a population declines. This happens when those entering the population through birth or immigration don't sufficiently replace those leaving through emigration or death.

The declining global population is perhaps the biggest cataclysmic event the human race is facing. It takes 2.1 children per woman of childbearing age for a nation's population to stay level. If the rate is higher than that, the population increases. If it is lower, then the population decreases. The 2.1 number takes into account factors such as infant mortality and the percentage of women who do not have children.[4]

Here's why:

1. Total Fertility Rate (TFR): The average number of babies per woman needs to be slightly above two in order to compensate for individuals who do not have children or die before reaching reproductive age. This is known as replacement level fertility. The single most important factor in population growth is the TFR. If, on average, women give birth to 2.1 children and these children survive to the age of fifteen, any given woman will have replaced herself and her partner upon death. A TFR of 2.1 is known as the replacement rate.[5]
2. Balancing birth and death rates: A birth rate of 2.1 helps to balance the birth rate with the death rate, ensuring that there are enough individuals to replace the older generation. If the birth rate falls below this level, the population will gradually decline over time.

When the birth rate falls below 2.1 babies per woman, several consequences can occur:

1. Aging population: With fewer births, the proportion of elderly individuals in the population increases. This can lead to a shrinking workforce and increased strain on social security systems.
2. Economic implications: A declining population can have negative impacts on the economy, as there are fewer people contributing to the workforce and consumer demand decreases. This can result in a decrease in economic growth and productivity.

3. Declining population size: Over time, if the birth rate remains consistently below 2.1, the population will continue to decline. This will have long-term implications for a country's demographics, infrastructure, and overall development.

Falling Fertility Rates

Falling birth rates are a major concern for some of Asia's biggest economies. China is a good example of population decline. New births in China are set to fall to record lows this year, demographers say, dropping below 10 million from last year's 10.6 million babies, which were already 11.5 percent lower than in 2020.[6] China's National Health Commission announced that it would take steps to reduce the number of abortions in the country. China's one-child abortion policy—which was recently modified to a two-, then a three-child policy—has led to a drop in the population and severe gender imbalance because of a traditional preference for male children and the selective abortion of female babies. There are now thirty million more men than women in China as a result of killing baby girls through abortion.[7]

South Korea's fertility rate, already the world's lowest, continued its dramatic decline in 2023, as women concerned about their career advancement and the financial cost of raising children decided to delay childbirth or to not have babies. The average number of expected babies for a South Korean woman during her reproductive life fell to a record low of 0.72 from 0.78 in 2022.[8]

Japan's population is projected to fall from a peak of 128 million in 2017 to less than fifty-three million by the end of the century. With their aging population, more adult diapers are sold in Japan than baby diapers. Italy is expected to see an equally dramatic population crash from sixty-one million to twenty-eight million over the same time frame. China, which used to be the most populous nation on Earth, has dropped to second place, behind India. China is expected to peak at 1.4 billion in four years' time before dropping to nearly 732 million by 2100, said a study led by an international team of researchers published in *The Lancet*.[9]

More than twenty countries, including Italy, Japan, Poland, Portugal, South Korea, Spain, and Thailand, will see their numbers diminish by at least half by the year 2100 according to projections in a major study.[10] By century's end, 183 of 195 countries, barring an influx of immigrants, will have fallen below the replacement threshold needed to maintain population levels.[11]

Cost of Population Decline

While it is difficult to quantify exactly how much policies fighting population decline have cost, South Korean President Yoon Suk-Yeol recently said his country had spent more than $200 billion (£160 billion) over the past sixteen years on trying to boost the population.[12] Governments in Asia are spending hundreds of billions of dollars trying to reverse the trend. Japan began introducing policies to encourage couples to have more children in the 1990s. South Korea started doing the same in the 2000s, while Singapore's first fertility policy dates back to 1987. China, which has seen its population fall for the first time in sixty years, recently joined the growing club. Researchers at the University of Washington's Institute for Health Metrics and Evaluation showed the global fertility rate was nearly cut in half in 2017 to 2.4, and their study, published in *The Lancet*, projects it will fall below 1.7 by 2100.[13]

According to new guidelines published on China's state-run commission's website, officials plan to offer incentives to encourage family growth, including expanding access to childcare services, reducing the cost of attending nursery school, and working with employers to make offices more "family friendly."[14] The Chinese government has also vowed to make infertility treatment more widely available to married women, by including reproductive technology in the country's national medical system. This is a drastic change from just a few years ago when the Chinese government was enforcing its one-child policy by aggressively forcing women to have abortions.

In neighboring Japan, which had record low births of fewer than 800,000 last year, Prime Minister Fumio Kishida has pledged to double the budget for child-related policies to just over 2 percent of the country's gross domestic product. Globally the number of countries wanting to increase fertility has more than tripled since 1976, according to the most recent report by the United Nations.[15]

Aging Populations

For many countries another issue is the rapidly aging population. Japan leads with nearly 30 percent of its population now over the age of sixty-five, and some other nations in the region are not far behind. And when the share of the working age population gets smaller, the cost and burden of looking after the non-working population grows. Negative population growth has a negative impact on the economy, and combined with an aging population, these countries won't be able to afford to support the elderly.

Since 1950, global average lifespans have increased by almost twenty-eight years (from 45.51 to 73.16 in 2023), accompanied by a decline in global fertility from an average of five births per woman in 1950 to 2.3 births per woman in 2021. Studies project that the number of under five-year-olds will fall from 681 million in 2017 to 401 million in 2100. The number of over eighty-year-olds will soar from 141 million in 2017 to 881 million in 2100.[16]

Reasons for Negative Population Growth

Aging Population
One of the reasons for the declining population is the aging demographic in many countries. As life expectancy increases due to advancements in healthcare and living standards, birth rates are

not keeping pace. This trend is observed in countries such as Japan, Germany, and Italy, where the proportion of elderly citizens is rapidly growing, resulting in a decline in the younger population. In 2022, there were 771 million people aged sixty-five-plus accounting for 10 percent of the world's population. Starting in 2073, there are projected to be more people aged sixty-five and older than under age fifteen—the first time this will be the case.[17]

Low Fertility Rates
Declining fertility rates play a vital role in the reduction of the global population.[18] Developed nations, including South Korea, Singapore, and Spain, are experiencing consistently low birth rates. Factors for the declining rates include an increasing number of abortions, increased use of contraceptives, young people delaying getting married, changing societal norms, and career aspirations for women.

Urbanization and Lifestyle Changes
Urbanization and lifestyle changes also impact declining population rates. As more people migrate from rural areas to cities, they tend to have fewer children due to increased education and career opportunities, higher living costs, and limited space.[19] Countries like China, Brazil, and Russia have observed a decline in population growth due to these factors.

Economic Factors
In countries with strong economies, the cost of raising children can be high, including expenses related to education, healthcare, and housing.[20] This financial burden, coupled with the desire for a higher standard of living, contributes to a decrease in birth rates. Countries like the United States, Canada, and Australia have experienced declining population growth due to economic factors. In many countries, couples are choosing better cars, homes, and clothes over having children.

Education

Universities and colleges have been strongly influenced by a Western way of thinking. They encourage young people to embrace a selfish attitude regarding independence and gaining more material goods while being very antagonistic toward families and children. This trend is evident in countries like Sweden and the Netherlands. There is a strong correlation between higher levels of education and lower number of childbirths.[21]

Migration

Migration can lead to a decline in the population of a particular country as people move to other countries in search of better opportunities.

Materialistic Mindset

Western materialistic thinking has had a significant impact on young people globally and has contributed to a decrease in childbirth rates.[22] There has been a growing emphasis on material possessions, career advancement, and individualistic pursuits. This focus on materialism has led to a shift in priorities, with many young people prioritizing personal satisfaction and material wealth over starting a family and having children. More people are either delaying marriage or not getting married at all, and having no children if they do get married or having only one child.

Sexual Confusion

Homosexuality and transgenderism have been fully embraced by the West and are being exported globally. In the U.S., 84 percent of adults aged eighteen to thirty-four support same-sex marriage. In 2017, 4.5 percent of adults in the U.S. identified as gay; this is up from 3.5 percent in 2012. Approximately 8 percent of adults who are eighteen to twenty-four now say they fall in the LGBTQ+ category. All of these choices add to the declining population through lack of reproduction.[23]

Birth Control

The widespread and increased use of contraceptives has played a significant role in the decline of birth rates globally.[24] This has led to a decrease in pregnancies and a reduction in the number of children being born. The shift toward contraceptive use has resulted in lower birth rates, contributing to demographic changes and influencing social, economic, and environmental factors on a global scale.

Abortions

There is a growing global trend toward legalizing or liberalizing abortion laws.[25] Since 2000, thirty-eight countries have changed their abortion laws, and all but Nicaragua expanded the legal grounds on which women can have an abortion. The seventy-three million babies killed by abortions each year is profound in terms of population decline. Each one of those children could have been born and created more babies. This means the total cost to humanity is hundreds of millions of lives lost.

Projected Outcomes of Negative Population Growth

1. Aging Population—The aging population can have a significant impact on the global economy.[26] While the younger generation does not reproduce, this means we end up with an inverted pyramid with fewer and fewer people supporting an ever growing number of elderly people. This is unsustainable. With a larger proportion of elderly individuals, there will be increased pressure on healthcare systems, social security programs, and pension funds. A higher proportion of elderly individuals will lead to a shrinking labor force. As the number of elderly individuals increases, there will be higher demands for healthcare services, long-term care facilities, and social services, such as home care. This will lead to challenges in providing adequate care and support for the aging population.

2. Labor Shortage—Declining population rates will lead to labor shortages in various sectors affecting economic productivity and growth.[27] Countries will face challenges in sustaining their workforce, resulting in increased dependency ratios and strain on social welfare systems.
3. Economic Collapse—As governments deal with the cumulative blows of increased expenses from providing for an aging population, fewer workers to drive economic engines, and lower income as a result of a shrinking tax base, we will see governments defaulting or in some cases collapsing.[28]

Africa Grows

Sub-Saharan Africa, meanwhile, will triple in size to some three billion people, with Nigeria alone expanding to almost 800 million people in 2100, second only to India's 1.1 billion.[29] For high-income countries facing shrinking populations, the best solutions for sustaining population levels and economic growth will be flexible immigration policies and social support for families who want children, *The Lancet* study concluded.[30]

Conclusion

The persistent historical trends mentioned have inescapable consequences in terms of population. Between 1950 and 2010, the populations of the rich regions of the North increased through net immigration, and since 1990 immigration has been the North's primary source of population growth. In Europe, immigration accounted for 80 percent of the population growth between 2000 and 2018, while in North America, it constituted 32 percent in that same period.

The bottom line is that only net immigration can ensure population stability or growth in the aging advanced economies of the North, and this will happen only if countries promote forward-looking immigration policies that allow larger numbers of immigrants to emigrate from countries with growing populations—and that means Africa.

By the year 2100, many countries will face the challenges of decreasing populations, aging populations, decreasing workforces, and a collapsing tax base. All around the world, the fertility rate is dropping below replacement level. With negative population growth, each generation produces fewer offspring, who produce fewer still, until there are none. There is a real possibility that governments will be at risk of default or even collapse altogether. Aging populations will lead to a higher dependency ratio, with fewer active workers supporting a larger number of retirees. This will place immense strain on government resources, including healthcare, pensions, and social security systems. With a shrinking workforce, tax revenues will decline, making it increasingly difficult for governments to meet the growing demands of an aging society. As a result, governments may struggle to fulfill their obligations, leading to financial instability, debt defaults, and potential collapse.

Countries with significantly declining populations, which will be most countries in the world, will have few possible solutions.

These solutions include:

1. Decrease the number of abortions.
2. Discourage the use of birth control.
3. Incentivize people to have babies.
4. Increase immigration.

Countries are already using immigration to boost their population and compensate for falling fertility rates. However, this stops being the answer once nearly every country's population is shrinking. We will go from a time where it's a choice to open borders, to intense competition for migrants. Lawmakers are already discussing changing their immigration laws to try to entice younger workers from overseas. Globally, the fertility rate is falling so fast that eventually countries will be competing to attract immigrants to come and work in their countries. And the one continent that will have the world's most sought after resource, people, will be Africa!

This chapter deals heavily with numbers and statistics. But as the story at the beginning of the chapter shows, it is people who pay the price, and more often than not, women. Satan's influence and impact on decreasing the population has done nothing to decrease the world's sinful sexual appetite. Quite the opposite. Sexual immorality is increasing as never before. And women, sometimes young girls in elementary school or younger, are sexually abused, enslaved, or trafficked by ravenous men who use them and then cast them aside, sometimes even murdering them. The World Health Organization estimates that one in three women experience physical or sexual violence in their lifetime.[31] The shrinking population will only be equaled by a growing sexual immorality and sexual abuse of women. But like the story in the beginning of this chapter illustrated, God stands ready to break every chain and set every captive free. And His chosen vessel for doing this is His Church—which means you and me!

Chapter 4:
Africa's Prophetic Mandate: Delivering Christ's Message of Life to the World

It's been fifteen years since the event, but I remember it like it was yesterday. Several of us had gathered from all around the world to seek the Lord's voice on a charter that would bind us together as ministry leaders involved with championing the sanctity of human life. As I was in prayer, I felt the Lord impress a word on my heart. He said, "The message of the sacredness of human life cannot be separated from the Great Commission charge to make disciples of all nations."

Immediately I wrote that down and passed it on to the leadership as my contribution to the charter known as the 72 Ransom Avenue Covenant. A few weeks later I was back in Kenya leading a seminar for pastors on the sanctity of human life. At the end of the training, a pastor stood there to share a prayer item in front of the whole congregation of eighty pastors.

"Brothers and sisters," he began. "You see, I'm a pastor, and I have been a pastor for over twenty years. It is my desire to see as many people as possible come to faith in Christ. However, there is one person I have never been able to pray for or share the Gospel with. I hold so much bitterness and anger against him, that I don't even wish to share the same heaven with him in the future." There was deep silence in the room as he continued.

"You see, in my tribe, when a woman gives birth to twins during her first pregnancy, it is considered a curse, so one of the children is supposed to be killed by the traditional midwives during delivery. My mother had twins for her first pregnancy. It was myself and my brother. When the midwives informed my father that it was twins, he immediately ordered the midwives to see to it that one of the babies did not make it alive. So my brother was killed, and I survived. This devastated my mother and changed her life forever. Instead of helping my mother through the grief, my father blamed her for the twins and the death of my brother and used this to turn so violent on my mother until he drove her out of our home, and then he married another woman. I have suffered alongside my mother throughout my childhood, and I have always been angry with my father. I know where he lives, but I have not visited him for all my years that I have been in ministry."

I asked how we could pray for him. "This message about the sanctity of human life has convicted me toward forgiveness and toward believing that my father is made in God's image and equally deserves the Gospel. Please pray for me to forgive him and go preach the Gospel to him." We prayed.

A week later, the pastor called me on the phone super excited that after changing his worldview on the sacredness of human life, he had started to see his dad through the lens of God's truth and had gone to visit him and share the Gospel with him. I could hear him jumping up and down saying, "I visited my father. We had a great conversation, and today he came to my church and gave his life to Jesus." When Church leaders embrace the message of life, the Gospel is advanced significantly.

Bramuel Musya
Africa Life Coordinator
Life Equip Global

This story is a great illustration of how proclaiming the message of life goes hand in hand with proclaiming the Gospel of Christ. Planting the seeds of the message of the sanctity of human life and God's command to defend innocent human life within the growing Church in Africa will have global implications. The growth of the Church in Africa will not stop at the borders of Africa. We see God blessing the African Church and allowing the Church to continue to expand until its impact will be felt by every nation on Earth.

As we look to the future, we know that negative population growth (NPG) will ravage close to a hundred countries, leaving them in a state of despair and uncertainty. This is not guesswork. This is math, and it *will* happen. Dozens of countries will see their populations cut in half. The world's population will age drastically. Many governments will be bankrupt or near collapse. However, in the middle of this chaos and turmoil, a surprising shift in power and influence will have taken place. Africa, with its rapidly growing population, will emerge as a primary economic and spiritual powerhouse on Earth.

As has been stated, when a nation is in NPG, its leadership has a limited number of options to improve the situation.

These include:

- Improve Birth Rates: Implement policies and initiatives, such as financial incentives or subsidies, to encourage couples to have more children.
- Extend Retirement Age: Increasing the retirement age can help soften the effects of negative population growth.
- Improve Healthcare: Improving healthcare systems and promoting a healthy lifestyle can ensure that people who are living longer live healthier and therefore more productive lives.
- Legalize Euthanasia: Euthanasia is the deliberate act of ending a person's life, in other words, killing the elderly. Just as China for many years enforced a one-child policy to limit population

growth, it is a possibility that governments would embrace euthanasia to limit the expense of providing for an aging population caused by population decline. Twenty-two countries have legalized euthanasia or are not enforcing laws against the killing of the elderly.
- Discourage the use of birth control, which is very unlikely.
- Discourage or make abortions illegal, which is also very unlikely.
- The number one solution to NPG is to *encourage immigration to offset the declining population.*

But when neighboring countries are also experiencing population decline, governments will have only one option: look to the one continent that is not experiencing NPG. That continent is Africa.

Over the past twenty years, Africa's population has experienced significant growth. According to data from the United Nations, the continent's population has increased from approximately 800 million in 2000 to over 1.4 billion in 2023.[1] This growth can be attributed to several factors. Advancements in healthcare and sanitation have led to a decline in mortality rates, particularly among infants and children. This has resulted in longer life expectancy and a larger population of reproductive age. Furthermore, factors like declining poverty rates, economic growth, and improved living conditions have also played a role in Africa's population expansion.

As NPG increases, countries from every corner of the globe will turn to Africa to help alleviate their declining population issues. Africans, renowned for their strong work ethic and resilience, will take up many duties in countries struggling to rebuild their economies. The once marginalized African continent will transform into a beacon of hope and progress.

The Church in Africa

The Church in Africa has witnessed unprecedented growth in recent years, making it *the fastest growing Church in the world!* As of 2023, there were an estimated 718 million Christians from all denominations in Africa. Assuming that the proportion of Christians remains relatively stable, the number of Christians in Africa could potentially surpass one billion by the end of the century. Christianity is embraced by the majority of the population in most southern African, southeast African, and central African states and others in large parts of the Horn of Africa and West Africa. Christians form 49 percent of Africa's population. In a relatively short time, Africa has risen from having a majority of followers of indigenous, traditional religions to being predominantly a continent of Christians and Muslims. The growing Church in Africa is the primary reason why Satan is focused on growing the Muslim faith in Africa, hoping that Africans embrace Islam before they ever hear about the Gospel of Christ.

Because God has blessed Africa with His presence and the Church in Africa is exploding in numbers—and with the world set to experience massive negative population growth—the stage is set for the Church in Africa to bring its message of Christ and life to the world! As African nations experience urbanization, globalization, and increased access to education, people are searching for meaning and stability in all of this rapid change. They are finding it in Jesus and the Church. The Christian Church in Africa is bringing the powerful Gospel of Jesus Christ to a hungry audience. It offers a vibrant and dynamic expression of Christianity, resonating with many Africans who seek a personal and transformative encounter with God. Its emphasis on personal salvation, biblical teachings, and spiritual renewal has attracted a vast number of followers across the continent. While addressing the spiritual and emotional needs of individuals and families, the Church is also providing a sense of community, purpose, and hope.

The rapid growth of the Church in Africa is a remarkable Holy Spirit-driven phenomenon. The blend of dynamic Spirit-filled worship and a focus on personal transformation has resonated with millions across the continent. As the Church continues to expand, it has the potential to shape the social, cultural, and spiritual landscape of Africa, bringing hope, healing, and empowerment to its followers, and to the world at large!

The Church in Africa has already emerged as a dynamic force in global Christianity, playing a significant role in starting churches all over the world. Some denominations are experiencing unprecedented growth and are already expanding beyond the borders of Africa, establishing churches around the world. This global expansion is driven by the passionate faith and dynamic worship characteristic of these churches, as well as their commitment to evangelism and social transformation. The statistics reveal the remarkable impact the African Church are having on the world.

While the Church is growing across the entire African continent, several countries stand out for their exceptional growth rates. These countries include:

1. Nigeria: With a population of over 200 million people, Nigeria is home to one of the largest Christian populations in Africa with 88.4 million Nigerians professing Christianity. The Church has experienced remarkable growth in Nigeria, particularly in urban areas where the influence of Pentecostalism is strong. Nigeria is expected to have the largest population on Earth by the year 2100.[2]
2. Kenya: Kenya has witnessed a surge in the number of evangelical churches, with charismatic movements gaining popularity. The emphasis on the Gospel and healing ministries has resonated with many Kenyans, leading to exponential growth. As of 2020, Kenya had a Christian population of roughly 44.5 million people, according to the source's projections. By 2030, this population is forecast to increase to 55.3 million individuals. Over 85 percent of the Kenyan population profess Christianity.[3]
3. Ghana: The Evangelical Church in Ghana has experienced

significant growth, driven by charismatic and Pentecostal movements. The emphasis on spiritual deliverance and vibrant worship has attracted a large following.

4. South Africa: South Africa has seen substantial growth in the Church. Of the sixty-two million people who live in South Africa, 78 percent (52.8 million) identified as Christians.[4] The fusion of African spirituality with charismatic Christianity has created a unique expression of faith, drawing in many South Africans.

According to recent data, there are over fifty million members of African Pentecostal churches worldwide. This number represents a significant increase from previous years and demonstrates the exponential growth of these churches. By establishing branches and networks of churches in Europe, North America, Asia, and other parts of the world, African Pentecostal churches have become a vibrant and influential force in global Christianity.

Another African denomination experiencing remarkable growth is the Anglican Church. According to statistics, the Anglican Communion in Africa has witnessed a substantial increase in membership over the past few decades. As of 2019, there were approximately forty million Anglicans in Africa, accounting for a significant portion of the global Anglican population. This growth can be attributed to the fervent evangelistic efforts of African Anglicans, who are passionate about sharing their faith and planting churches both within their own countries and abroad.

The Anglican Church in Africa has also been proactive in establishing networks of churches globally. Through initiatives such as the Anglican Global Mission Partnerships, African Anglican churches have formed partnerships with churches in other parts of the world. These partnerships facilitate the exchange of resources, training, and support, enabling the establishment of new churches in various regions. The Anglican Church in Africa has been particularly active in starting churches in Europe, North America, and other parts of the global South.

Furthermore, the Anglican Church in Africa has demonstrated remarkable adaptability and innovation in spreading the Gospel. African Anglican leaders have recognized the importance of sharing the message of Christ within different cultural contexts. This approach has allowed the Church to effectively engage with diverse communities and establish churches that are relevant and impactful. By incorporating African cultural expressions and values into their worship and ministry, the Anglican Church in Africa has been able to connect with people from different backgrounds and effectively share the message of salvation.

The Baptist Church in Africa has also experienced significant growth in recent years, in terms of membership and influence both within the continent and beyond. The number of Baptist church members in Africa has been steadily increasing. From 1990 to 2019, the total Baptist membership in Africa rose from approximately five million to over fifteen million, reflecting a threefold increase.

As negative population growth increases and more and more Christian Africans leave their homeland to help an ailing world, they will bring with them their deep faith in Christ and their unshakable belief in the sanctity of human life. The world is hungry for hope, and hope is what they will get from the men and women of Africa. As God's hand leads them, our prayer and hope is that they will be bold in sharing the message that *all* life matters *because all* life is made in the image of God. We also pray and hope that as the members of the Church from Africa bring the Gospel message to the world, that revival, perhaps the world's last great revival, will break out. The stage will then be set for the return of the King!

In the heart of Africa, a magnificent river emerges, carving its way through the vast and diverse landscape. Born from the union of two mighty streams—the Blue Nile and the White Nile—the Nile River begins its majestic journey. The Blue Nile, originating from the highlands of Ethiopia, cascades down the rugged terrain, while the White Nile flows gently from the Great Lakes of East Africa. These two powerful forces merge in Sudan, giving rise to the life-giving Nile. Spanning over 4,000 miles, the Nile winds its way through eleven countries, leaving its mark on the lands of Ethiopia, Sudan, South Sudan, Uganda, Egypt, Tanzania, Rwanda, Burundi, Congo-Kinshasa, Kenya, and Eritrea.

Before the Nile River became the mighty force we know today, its journey began as a network of insignificant small streams and creeks that meander through the African landscape. From the Ethiopian highlands, a multitude of rivulets and tributaries trickle down, each contributing to the growing power of the Nile. Streams like the Atbara, the Tekezé, and the Sobat, among many others, weave their way through the rugged terrain, gathering strength and nourishment along the way. These humble beginnings, hidden among the vast wilderness, are the lifeblood of the Nile, nurturing its growth and setting the stage for the grandeur that lies ahead. Every small stream and creek plays a vital role in the formation of this legendary river.

How do these streams become a mighty river? Every stream or creek that sends its waters into the Nile makes a tiny addition to the whole, but when taken together, the multiplier effect is massive. Along its 4,135-mile journey, the stream becomes a force of nature. The Nile's power comes from the many streams and brooks that join it along the way.

The Church could be like the Nile. The Church is composed of people, great and small, but all equal in God's sight and all filled with His Holy Spirit. Like the many streams that make up the Nile, the Church is composed of tiny, small, medium, and large churches. It is made up of the many denominations, the Anglicans and Baptists and Catholics and Charismatics and Orthodox and Presbyterians, who know and worship God. It is made up of the many NGOs and ministries that serve the needy and the poor. But too often the Church acts like strangers to one another. Church pastors won't speak to each other. NGOs don't cooperate. Denominations spend more time attacking each other than working together.

Did you know that Jesus prayed for us over 2,000 years ago? Jesus said,

> My prayer is not for them alone. I pray also for those *who will believe in me* through their message, that all of them may be one, Father, just as you are in me and I am in you. May they also be in us so that the world may believe that you have sent me. I have given them the glory that you gave me, that they may be one as we are one—I in them and you in me—so that they may be brought to complete unity. Then the world will know that you sent me and have loved them even as you have loved me. (John 17:20-23)

Jesus prayed that we may be one. Unity is Jesus' desire for His Church, and when we start working together, instead of against each other, then we become like the Nile, with each of our streams adding to the whole and becoming an unstoppable force. A force of goodness and mercy and grace and abundance and LIFE! A force against which the gates of hell itself cannot stand! And that is God's vision for the Church in Africa!

When the streams that form the Nile join together, they stop being the streams from Ethiopia, Sudan, South Sudan, Uganda, Egypt, Tanzania, Rwanda, Burundi, Congo-Kinshasa, Kenya, and Eritrea. When the streams join together, they are no longer a stream. They are a part of the Nile. In fact, they *are* the Nile! Currently the Church in Africa, and around the world, is not marching in step. We have let man's opinions, denominations, or boundaries prevent us from joining together. But if the believers in Ethiopia and Kenya and Zambia and South Africa and in all fifty-four countries of Africa join their "streams" together, then Africa will be united. The Church in Africa will be one, as Jesus prayed we would be. And Africa will fulfill its promise, and the whole world will be blessed!

> I will surely bless you, and I will surely multiply your offspring as the stars of heaven and as the sand that is on the seashore. And your offspring shall possess the gate of his enemies, and in your offspring shall all the nations of the earth be blessed, because you have obeyed my voice. (Genesis 22:17-18, ESV)

The African Awakening prophetically informs us of how abortion has multiplied around the world, how negative population growth is going to cause economic devastation, and how the world will come to Africa seeking immigrants as a solution to their demographic crisis. *The African Awakening* is also a story of God's redeeming love for a lost and hurting world. The Lord has placed His hand of blessing on the Church in Africa. The explosive growth of the Church in Africa is God's doing, God's blessing, not man's. This blessing is not meant to be kept in one city, one country, or even in one continent. The blessing God has poured upon the Church in Africa is meant to be a blessing to a lost and hurting world. God has allowed situations to occur around the world that put Africa on the path to a historic opportunity. Like the Nile River, the many Christian denominations, Christian schools, churches, ministries, and Christian NGOs in Africa, when working together, can become an unstoppable force for good. A force that the Lord can use to transform not only the continent of Africa, but to share the Gospel of Christ and the message of life with a lost and hurting world.

Just as small streams can turn into a mighty river, the seeds we plant can have explosive growth. "Still other seed fell on good soil, where it produced a crop—a hundred, sixty or thirty times what was sown" (Matthew 13:8). Jesus said, "And I tell you, you are Peter, and on this rock I will build my church, and the gates of hell shall not prevail against it" (Matthew 16:18, ESV). The Church is made up of simple believers, filled with the Holy Spirit, who can accomplish amazing feats. We make up the body of Christ. And God has promised us that we will defeat hell. But like the Israelites wandering in the wilderness, we need to have the courage to enter into the Promised Land, knowing that the Lord will lead us and will defeat the enemies we will face.

How will the Church in Africa be turned into a global powerhouse for life? The accomplishment of God's prophetic promise for Africa begins with Christians in Africa becoming equipped with powerful biblical truth to combat Satan's Global Abortion Genocide. And in order to become equipped, Christians need to be taught. Several years ago I was teaching pastors in India. For four days, I taught the biblical principles on the sanctity of human life. Once we finished, I returned to the United States.

I returned to India recently where Simon and Johanna Durairaj, the leaders of Life For All, had been sharing what they had been taught twelve years earlier. After launching Life For All and multiplying the message of the sanctity of human life throughout all of India, and seeing pro-life ministries multiply throughout the land, they informed me that 39,000 babies have been saved from abortion! God had created a bountiful harvest. Just imagine the harvest that will happen as the message of life multiplies through Africa led by the world's largest Christian Church. When the Lord directs us to plant seeds, we have to trust Him for the harvest.

Life Equip Global has been called to equip the global Church with a message of life. This is a huge vision that will take God's strategy to accomplish, especially in Africa. This strategy includes scheduling regional meetings with global movement leaders where we will help them catch fire for sharing the sanctity of human life. Global movement leaders are individuals who hold significant leadership roles within the Christian community, specifically in relation to denominations, groups of churches, or networks on a global scale.

These global movement leaders are characterized by their ability to inspire and mobilize people toward a common vision and mission. They possess a deep understanding of the cultural, social, and theological nuances within the diverse Christian landscape, enabling them to effectively navigate and bridge different perspectives and practices. Global movement leaders are committed to fostering unity, collaboration, and growth within their respective spheres of influence, working toward the advancement of the Gospel and the expansion of the Kingdom of God. Their leadership is marked by a strong emphasis on discipleship, equipping and empowering others, and promoting a global perspective in Christian ministry and mission.

These global movement leaders—once they catch the passion for the message of life—will provide the African Life Coordinator, Bramuel Musya from Kenya, the opportunity to schedule regional trainings throughout Africa to train and equip national trainers in each country. These national trainers will offer *prevention, intervention, and restoration training* and seminars throughout Africa. Through this strategy, millions of African believers will be equipped and prepared to embrace the message of life, make it a reality in their lives and families, and multiply the message of life wherever the Lord may take them.

When the message of life has been shared and multiplied throughout Africa, when it becomes a part of the very fiber of the Church, then it will be passed down from one generation to the next. In so doing, the Church in Africa will be a huge blessing to the continent of Africa and will be prepared for the day when the nations of the world come knocking. On that day, the people of Africa will venture out to help the many nations with shrinking populations. They will bring with them their many skills as teachers, doctors, engineers, and laborers. They will also bring their faith in Christ and knowledge of the Word of God. This will include the truth about the sanctity of human life that will have been passed down from one generation of Christians to another. When the people of Africa are received and welcomed by the nations of the world, the most valuable resource they will bring with them is their anointed teaching. This teaching, empowered by the Holy Spirit, will be exactly what the nations need to hear. This teaching will include:

- Repent from your sins and turn back to God, for only in Him will you find the solutions to all your problems.
- Only through faith in Jesus will your sins be forgiven and your relationship with God restored.
- Embrace and honor God's marriage covenant.
- Be fruitful and multiply, for that is God's command.
- Be respectful of sex and sexuality and use it appropriately in marriage.
- Stop killing your babies.

Like what occurred with my Maasai friends in Kenya, Africans first need to hear the truth about the sanctity of human life. Then there needs to be repentance for our past sins of spilling innocent blood of preborn children. Then we need to confess our sins and allow the Holy Spirit to come and heal our wounds. Then we can enter into a period of rejoicing as the Lord breaks every chain of shame and guilt.

I invite you to join us on this transformative journey that holds the potential to reshape the future of our global community. In a time when the killing of millions of babies by abortion is multiplying around the world, it is crucial that we rise up and address the pressing challenges that lie ahead. By partnering together—by uniting—we have the opportunity to fight the Global Abortion Genocide and bring about a world that embraces the sanctity of human life.

This world as we know it is going to change drastically. The goal for Christians should not be to try to hold back the inevitable, but to be prepared to use the cataclysmic changes about to take place as an opportunity to multiply the Gospel of Jesus Christ and the importance of sharing the message of the sanctity of human life. Let us seize this moment to empower a vision of the Church in Africa embracing the sanctity of human life, transforming the continent of Africa, and teaching the world to look to Christ as our only answer. By allowing the Father, the Son, and the Holy Spirit to guide our steps, and by uniting as one, we can turn this vision into a reality, ensuring a future where the sanctity of human life is cherished and celebrated worldwide while preparing for the return of the King.

Chapter 5:
Marriage: The Covenant for Life

At a training for pastors in Kenya, I experienced some culture shock. I was teaching a large group of Maasai pastors and their wives, who have a rich cultural heritage that is deeply rooted in their traditional beliefs and practices. Despite the influence of the Church, many Maasai pastors continue to uphold their cultural traditions, including their beliefs about the roles of husbands and wives.

In Maasai society, the roles of husbands and wives are clearly defined. The husband is traditionally seen as the provider and protector of the family. He is responsible for herding livestock, which is a central aspect of Maasai culture and economy. On the other hand, the wife's role in Maasai culture is primarily focused on the domestic sphere. She takes care of the household chores, such as cooking, cleaning, and taking care of the children.

In the crowded room where I was teaching, all the women sat on one side of the room and all the men on the other side. At this point in the training I was teaching about the five love languages and how important it is to know our wife's love language, whether it be acts of service, words of affirmation, receiving gifts, quality time, or physical touch. After explaining that my wife, Chris' love language was acts of service, I then shared that I sometimes help her with housework because that is her love language. Due to our cultural differences, I knew they would be surprised by me sharing this with them.

One pastor raised his hand and started by saying, "Pastor Raúl, you don't understand our culture." I immediately responded, "You are absolutely correct; please help me understand your culture." He then told me something that truly shocked me. He said, "Pastor Raúl, in our Maasai culture we show our wives we love them by beating them." I was positive that I misheard what he said, so I responded, "You know as an American, I sometimes have a hard time understanding words that are being said, especially as my accent is different from yours. Would you mind repeating what you said?" He said again, "In my culture, we show our wives we love them by beating them." I couldn't believe my ears. One last time I asked, "Please forgive me, but could you please repeat that one last time?" He was getting quite exasperated with me and stated quite forcefully, "I'm telling you, man, in my culture we show our wives we love them by beating them!!!" He continued, "Just last week a wife came to me to complain about her husband. She said she didn't think her husband loved her anymore because he had stopped beating her." That is when I realized how blindly following the culture of the country we come from can be damaging to our marriages.

Raúl Reyes
President
Life Equip Global

Marriage

Marriage, as God intended it, is a lifelong commitment; it is a union of two individuals who become one flesh. It is a bond of love, trust, and selflessness. Just as Christ loves the Church and gave Himself up for her, husbands are called to love their wives sacrificially—not beat them. And wives are called to respect and submit to their husbands, just as the Church submits to Christ. It is of primary importance that the Church embraces a true biblical understanding of marriage and teaches what the Bible has to say about marriage to their congregation. Only then will husbands and wives learn that God has a much better plan for them than what their culture has in mind.

Marriage was the first human institution God created. Two persons coming together with God at the center is God's design for marriage. This reflects the triune nature of God—the Father, Son, and Holy Spirit. God's Word tells us that everything that exists was made by God and belongs to God. Genesis 1 states, "In the beginning God created the heavens and the earth" (Genesis 1:1). This powerful statement makes clear that every atom that exists comes from the mind of God. God spoke everything into existence; therefore, everything that exists belongs to Him. "The earth is the LORD's and everything in it" (Psalm 24:1). God not only created matter and life—He also created the institutions by which man is governed and by which we flourish. This includes the institution of marriage and family.

Marriage is a divinely architected cathedral that radiates the majesty of God. It is a visible sign of God's love and grace in the world. In this sacred union, couples are called to love and cherish each other, to support and encourage one another, and to grow together in faith and love. They are called to be faithful and committed, honoring their vows and seeking to build a home filled with love, peace, and joy. Just as God created Eve and presented her to Adam, He continues to bless marriages today. Couples who embrace the divine purpose of marriage find strength, comfort, and fulfillment in their union. They become a testimony of God's love for His people, a reflection of the intimate relationship between Christ and the Church.

Marriage is more than just an arrangement between two individuals. Marriage is one man and one woman committed to each other before God for as long as they both shall live. It is a covenant before God and is the single most important human bond. A covenant is a legal binding contract made before God. Marriage is a lifetime covenant of companionship for the good of man and the glory of God. *Covenant* as defined by the Scriptures is a relationship which is meant to last a lifetime. If the human race were to embrace biblical marriage, and adhere to the commands the Lord has given us regarding marriage, we would eliminate unplanned pregnancies, STDs, rape, sexual abuse, divorce, and abortion. But this can only occur when the Church teaches *all* that God has taught us in His Word regarding marriage.

According to the Bible, God Himself created marriage in the Garden of Eden when He married Adam and Eve. We read,

> And the rib that the LORD God had taken from the man he made into a woman and brought her to the man. Then the man said, "This at last is bone of my bones and flesh of my flesh; she shall be called Woman, because she was taken out of Man." Therefore a man shall leave his father and his mother and hold fast to his *wife*, and they shall become one flesh. (Genesis 2:22-24, ESV, emphasis added).

God Himself brought Eve to Adam. In Genesis 2:18, we learn that God saw that it was not good for man to be alone. He chose to make a wife for Adam. Becoming husband and wife was not a decision they made on their own. God created and ordained marriage between one man and one woman.

Marriage is a holy covenant before God. And when we break that covenant, God will not accept our worship. "You ask, 'Why?' It is because the LORD is the witness between you and the wife of your youth. You have been unfaithful to her, though she is your partner, the wife of your *marriage covenant*" (Malachi 2:14, emphasis added).

Pastor Jack Hayford wrote,

The covenant of marriage is the single most important human bond that holds all of God's work on the planet together. It is no small wonder that the Lord is passionate about the sanctity of marriage and the stability of the home. This covenant of marriage is based on the covenant God has made with us. It is in the power of His promise to mankind that our personal covenant of marriage can be kept against the forces that would destroy homes and ruin lives.[1]

We read in God's Word, "But because there is so much sexual immorality, each man should have his own wife, and each woman should have her own husband" (1 Corinthians 7:2, NLT).

Marriage is a picture for the world to see the relationship of Christ to the Church. "'For this reason a man will leave his father and mother and be united to his wife, and the two will become one flesh.' This is a profound mystery—but I am talking about Christ and the church" (Ephesians 5:31-32). This picture of Christ's relationship with the Church allows us to mirror God's image. The Hebrew word for *mirror* means "to reflect God, to magnify, exalt, and glorify Him." Through the family, we can be God's representatives to a world that desperately needs to see who He is.

God in His Word says, "Marriage should be honored by all, and the marriage bed kept pure, for God will judge the adulterer and all the sexually immoral" (Hebrews 13:4). The word *all* means *everybody*—married and unmarried, believer and unbeliever.

Marriage is:

- Where husbands learn to love their wives.
- Where wives learn to respect their husbands.
- Where children are created, protected, nurtured, and raised.
- Where children learn about God.

Satan Hates Marriage

Satan, the enemy, hates marriage. Marriage was God's idea for the human race which is why He created Eve. Destroying a Christian marriage is often one of the most effective weapons to weaken the sanctity of marriage and undermine a growing church, successful ministry, or other Christian project. We so often hear of ministries collapsing because the leader had an affair with another woman—or man.

Jesus told us that Satan comes only to steal, kill, and destroy. As most people from a broken marriage will testify, divorce steals our joy, kills the hope of a future together, and destroys lives. If Satan can break up your marriage, he goes a long way toward stealing, killing, and destroying large parts of your life, peace, and happiness. In addition, it will also negatively affect the lives of many other people in your life, especially your children.

The destruction of marriage really is a win-win situation for the enemy. It hurts people and attacks God, and as such he is prepared to invest quite a lot of energy and resources into it. One of the ways Satan is trying to destroy marriage is by redefining marriage. Many Christians foolishly believe that same-sex marriage is the enemy's ultimate goal in the fight to redefine marriage. The truth is that same-sex marriage is just *another step* in the process to erase the boundaries of what constitutes marriage and family altogether.

The assault against the sanctity of marriage is a satanic attack aimed at destroying one of God's primary building blocks for society. While the rejection of God and His Word leads to worship of self, pride, and selfishness, the rejection of biblical marriage is leading us toward rebelliousness and a rejection of all biblical truth.

The Lord has given us the Church, godly men and women, marriage, and the family as lifeguards against a deadly and dangerous world with a dangerous enemy intent on drowning us in a sea of destruction, disaster, and death. Godly men and women, taught in a Bible-preaching church, raise up godly children. Godly families bless the communities in which they live and act as lifeguards against the evil spreading throughout the land.

The Family

The biblical family usually consists of one man and one woman, married before God for life. It also includes their children, either through natural birth or adoption. Families can be complex as death, divorce, or disease impact Christian marriages. Families often include extended family members, with aunties or grandfathers sometimes leading the family in the absence of fathers and mothers. When practiced as God designed, the family will establish the foundation for a healthy, loving, and complete society—the society God intended for His glory. The family begins with God, is formed and guided by God, and is given to man for enjoyment and fulfillment, created to be a vehicle for God to fulfill His plan for creation and the completion of His Kingdom on Earth.

The family unit is God's basic foundation for civil society. If every family lived according to God's design, society within every culture could be creative, productive, fulfilling, sustaining, and peaceful. It could be a world without poverty, violence, and misery. All of our potential for good can be fully realized within the family as we allow Christ to rule in our hearts and then express this kind of love to each other.

In every culture, society, and nation, the family holds a special importance. God loves, cares for, and provides for us through families. He has granted authority for families to function according to His design. God's design for the family is without equal and is not replaceable by any other social institution, for nowhere else are human beings better equipped to live together in harmonious, lifelong, loving relationships. By attempting to undermine and destroy the family, the Evil One seeks to destroy the very fabric the Lord has created, through which His blessings flow. All that exists should seek to have Christ at the center. That includes our nations, our communities, our churches, and our families. Everything we do or say should acknowledge and bring us closer to understanding Christ as the center of all things. This includes marriage.

God designed marriage with the intention of helping us become more holy and more like Christ—not with the intention of making us happier. There is something much more profound in the heart of God than simply to make us happy. It is to make us more like His Son, Jesus. Through marriage we can learn about unconditional love, respectful honor, how to forgive, and how to be forgiven. We can see our shortcomings and grow from that insight. We can develop a servant's heart and draw closer to God. We can protect against abortion—the unlawful taking of preborn human life. We can raise up a family that honors God and brings about life-transforming change in those we influence. As a result, true understanding of our purpose in life can be achieved, and we can live in joy, loving God, loving our family, and loving others.

The family is (or should be):

- Where husbands learn to love their wives.
- Where wives learn to respect their husbands
- Where children are created, protected, nurtured, raised, and instructed
- Where children come to know Jesus and the Bible.
- Where we learn to value the elderly.
- Where we learn how to be caring and compassionate toward others.
- Where boundaries and guidelines are established.
- Where we learn about life and death.
- Where we learn about biblical sexuality.
- Where we learn discipline and selflessness.
- Where we learn the importance of serving others.
- Where we live out the principles taught in the Bible.

Family and Culture

Culture is the beliefs, customs, values, and behaviors that characterize a group or society. It has powerfully affected how we act or think since the beginning of time—as seen in the story of the Maasai pastor who was taught that beating his wife was a way of showing affection. Culture affects how we treat each other and helps explain why we treat others poorly, injuring them or even killing them because of color, gender, race, or nationality dating back thousands of years. The story at the beginning of this chapter is a great example of culture infiltrating and perverting what God intended for marriage. Regardless of how strong a cultural belief or behavior is, and regardless of how many generations it has been practiced, if it is contrary to God's commands—it is wrong! And beating your wife (or your husband) is absolutely wrong!

In the Bible, the Jews had a racist hostility toward Samaritans. In today's Africa, hostility between people of various tribes still exists and goes back hundreds of years. In India, the caste system still has Dalits ostracized and placed at the bottom of their society. In many countries, women are still treated as second-class citizens and many are being sold as sexual slaves, and slavery goes on to this very day. These are all wrong and stand against the sanctity of human life.

Being pro-life means when the culture of our country goes against God's culture, we must adopt the culture of the Kingdom of God and reject the culture of the country in which we live. As ambassadors of God's Kingdom we should treat all people with equal love and respect regardless of what our culture says. Being pro-life also has everything to do with how we treat our spouses, our children, our families, our neighbors, and all in our community.

The biblical values that come from the Word of God must always be greater than cultural beliefs we may have—from our tribe, our nation, or our continent. While culture, with all of its amazing gifts of customs, music, language, food, architecture, clothing, and more, is a wonderful, life-enriching part of all of us, we must always remember that as followers of Christ, our citizenship is in heaven. We are only temporary residents of this world, and we are called to expand God's Kingdom here, going into all the nations to proclaim Christ as Messiah.

The primary culture to which we belong is the culture of the Kingdom of God, and this is the culture we should want to see embraced and multiplied on the Earth—God's culture of love, compassion, truth, justice, and mercy. Every nation on Earth has embraced and recognized a family unit, complete with rules and expectations of how that family unit is to behave in order to produce a healthy society. But there are times in every culture when the human expectation of family is at odds with God's expectation of family—such as the beating of our wives. In this case, we must always choose the culture of the Kingdom of God versus the culture in which we live. When our culture's view of marriage and family is in line with the Word of God, we are blessed. When our culture's practice of marriage and family is different from God's design, when we replace God's truth with human tradition or experience, we step outside of His will and risk the consequences of a life outside of His plan. When we treat our wives (or husbands) differently than how God would have us love and honor our spouses, we dishonor God and our spouses, and break God's command.

As believers, we must remember that biblical truths should always be more deeply held than cultural beliefs and practices. We must not allow the love, mercy, and compassion of the Christian model of marriage to be replaced with the domination, rebellion, and fear that marks so many marriages and families in the world.

Too often our cultures defend or overlook behaviors that are clearly against the Word of God. Issues that many countries are dealing with include:

- A view of women and children as property.
- Allowing sexual immorality, including adultery, fornication, and pornography.
- Physical and sexual abuse of spouses and children.
- Allowing and encouraging child marriage (often for financial gain).
- Allowing marriage of one man to multiple wives.
- Homosexuality and other distortions of biblically established sex roles.
- The killing of babies through abortion.

It is our duty to maintain allegiance to God's Word and to promote a culture of life, even if it means we stand and speak out against our own culture. Cultures that often abuse women, exploit children, ignore the elderly, and abort the preborn. As believers, we must put God's Word into action in our lives, marriages, families, and churches, but this won't be possible unless we know the Word, which can only be accomplished through being a student of the Word of God. By doing so, the Word of God will start changing us so we can change our cultures to reflect the culture of the Kingdom of God.

Marriage and Sex

Only when two people are married are they free to know each other completely and that includes sexually—and as a result receive the blessing of children who would fill the Earth. The choice of sex is just that: a choice. And the Church must teach that that choice must be reserved for marriage. We must also teach that that choice may lead to the conception of a child, and we must never end the life of that child through abortion, whether the child was planned or not.

We all have a sexual drive. When our sexual drive is properly channeled in marriage, women and men can be cocreators of life, offering a place where our children can be raised in a loving family.

Men are called by God to be protectors of life. But when men are not properly taught to respect and protect their sexuality until marriage, instead of protectors they can become predators, ravenously taking whatever they desire. Sex as God designed brings life. Sex outside of God's design brings pain, heartache, and death, often through abortion.

The Benefits of Marriage

Marriage provides many benefits, rights, and protections. Marriage provides spiritual, physical, sexual, emotional, and social benefits, rights, and protections. Besides love, sexual intimacy, and companionship, marriage is how we create the legal family arrangement that is recognized by most countries around the world. Marriage is how we create a lifetime relationship that creates the stable environment most likely to foster long-term emotional, spiritual, and economic well-being.

Marriage is the God-ordained method in which we bring children into the world—prepared to be loved by a mother and father. Our family heritage is how the Lord blesses us—financially and spiritually—and how we inherit and distribute wealth. Many studies have found that marriage offers emotional, financial, and health benefits over those who are single or are living with someone outside of marriage.

Benefits of a Healthy Marriage to Children
- Less likely to have an abortion.
- Less likely to be raised in poverty.
- More likely to succeed academically.
- More likely to seek wisdom from God.
- More likely to have a good relationship with parents.
- Less likely to become pregnant—or impregnate someone.
- Less likely to abuse drugs and to commit delinquent behavior.
- Less likely to be sexually active as teenagers and contract an STD.

Benefits of a Healthy Marriage to Women
- Physically healthier.
- Emotionally healthier.
- Less likely to commit suicide.
- Benefits of becoming a mother.
- Less likely to end up in poverty.
- Decreased risk of alcohol or drug abuse.
- Have better relationships with their children.
- Less likely to be victim of domestic violence or sexual assault.

Benefits of a Healthy Marriage to Men
- Longer life.
- Intimacy with his wife.
- Greater financial stability.
- The benefit of becoming a father.
- Physically and mentally healthier.
- Increased stability of employment.
- Helps men mature into godly men.
- A help-meet to help live out God's design.
- Encouragement and love that promotes well-being.

The Role of the Husband and Father

The husband is required to love his wife as Christ loved the Church. Although men and women are equal in relationship to Christ, the Bible gives specific roles to each in marriage.

> Wives, submit yourselves to your own husbands as you do to the Lord. For the husband is the head of the wife as Christ is the head of the church, his body, of which he is the Savior. Now as the church submits to Christ, so also wives should submit to their husbands in everything. Husbands, love your

wives, just as Christ loved the church and gave himself up for her to make her holy, cleansing her by the washing with water through the word. (Ephesians 5:22-26)

These verses provide the guidelines for husbands and wives in a Christian family. The husband is required to love his wife as Christ loved the Church, and a wife should respect and submit to her husband and accept his leadership in the family. The husband is to be the spiritual leader in the home (1 Corinthians 11:3; Ephesians 5:23). This leadership should reflect Christ's leadership of and love for the Church. The husband's role starts with spiritual matters, helping lead the family into biblical truth. Fathers are instructed to bring up their children in the training and instruction of the Lord (Ephesians 6:4). He is also commanded to provide for his family. If he does not, "he has denied the faith and is worse than an unbeliever" (1 Timothy 5:8, ESV).

This does not mean that the wife cannot assist in supporting the family, for Proverbs 31 demonstrates that a godly wife may surely do so. God's Word is very clear on how a husband should treat his wife. Christian husbands are commanded to love their wives the way Jesus loved the Church, but what does this look like?

Husbands must love their wives:

- **Sacrificially**—"Husbands, love your wives, even as Christ also loved the church, and gave himself for it" (Ephesians 5:25, KJV).
- **Unconditionally**—Christ's love for the Church was and is unconditional. This means that His love is not dependent on what we do; it's dependent on who He is.
- **Tenderly**—"For no one has ever hated his own body, but he nourishes and tenderly cares for it, as the Messiah does the church" (Ephesians 5:29, ISV)

Husbands are commanded by the Bible to love their wives. If this were something that came naturally, it would not need to be a command. Love comes more naturally to women than to men, which is why the same passage commands women to respect their husbands, a task that comes less naturally to them than loving their husbands. Often when our wives are unhappy or dissatisfied, it may be because we husbands are not loving them in a godly manner, or loving them enough. A wife whose husband showers love upon her is a wife who will gladly return that love and may find it easier to show him the honor and respect she is commanded to give to him.

Often a husband also has the duty and responsibility (and privilege) of being a father. The role of father can be a double-edged sword. From fathers, we learn the fear of God, the importance of studying Scripture, and the character traits that help us to succeed in life. But from our fathers, many of us learned fear, intimidation, neglect, irresponsibility, addictions, sexual immorality, and violence. Children, especially boys, are hardwired to copy their fathers; they want to do whatever daddy does. Men of God must realize that they are constantly being watched by their children and that their children are copying what the fathers are doing. The highest form of discipling happens in the home between a father and his children. The seeds we plant in the hearts of our children will grow roots and influence their every action. This is why it is so important that we plant the Word of God in our children's hearts from an early age.

The Bible says a father is to be diligent in instructing his children in the ways and words of the Lord. "Train a child in the way that he should go, and when he is old he will not turn from it" (Proverbs 22:6, NET). It is a father's job—not the school's, not society's, not even the Church's—it is the father's job to train a child in the way he should go.

When a father and mother raise godly young men and women, communities can be blessed. When parents raise children who are undisciplined, ungodly, and rebellious, communities can be cursed. The primary responsibility for the number of unwanted pregnancies we are seeing around the world—and in Africa—lies at the feet of men. It is men who most often initiate sexual activity.

After their sexual activity results in a pregnancy, men are often unwilling to support the child they have created, which often leaves the young mother feeling abandoned and wondering how she can deal with her circumstances. He may also pressure her to abort the child because he is unwilling to embrace the responsibility of providing for that child. But young unmarried people are by no means the source of all abortions. Abortions after an unplanned pregnancy also occur within marriage often because of the fear of not being able to provide for the child due to poverty.

It is a father's role to be a godly and faithful husband to one wife, to obey the words that God used to describe marriage: "Therefore what God has joined together, let no one separate" (Mark 10:9). In this type of home, a child will be more likely to have confidence that his home will always be a safe and secure one. In this home, a child grows up knowing his or her place in the world, understanding that his or her life has purpose.

It is a father's role to treat his wife with love and respect. In this type of home, a young man grows up knowing that he is to treat women in the same manner modeled by his father. In this type of home, a young man learns that sexual intimacy is to be practiced only inside a God-ordained marriage. In this type of home, a young woman grows up knowing that her future husband should treat her the same way her father treats her mother. She should have no need to find sexual fulfillment in the arms of a young man before she is married, for she is content with the love she receives from her father. When a father reflects God's truth in his life, he becomes a pillar of strength that impacts his children through which the whole world is blessed.

The Christian husband and father can be an instrument of grace in God's hand. Men must be constantly aware of the high calling they have, with the support and partnership of their wives, to create God-centered families and raise up the next generation of men and women who will expand the Kingdom of God.

The Role of a Wife and Mother

The wife is required to respect and submit to her husband. Husbands and wives are equal in dignity and worth, but each has a different role to play and different obligations to fulfill. God created women to be helpmates, complements to men. When God created the world, He looked at everything He created and said that it was good, until the point when He created man and said that it was not good for man to be alone. He then created a woman.

God intends for all believers to submit to each other, to put each other first. In marriage, women are reminded to submit to and respect their husbands. This is something that all followers of Christ must do because we love and trust Jesus, and because we desire to keep His commands. But just as a husband is told to love his wife unconditionally, so is his wife told to respect and submit to her husband.

"But every husband must love his wife as he loves himself, and wives should respect their husbands" (Ephesians 5:33, GW). When a wife shows her husband unconditional respect, this will make him feel like the warrior that he longs to be. This will also motivate him to show her the kind of unconditional love that she desires, and she will be the treasured pearl that she has always longed to be. The combination of husbands showing love and wives showing respect will establish the proper foundation for happiness and for mutual blessing in marriage, as God continues the good work He has begun and brings it to completion in the relationship of marriage.

In addition to being a wife, many women have the added blessing of becoming a mother. The women whom the Lord blesses with children should take that responsibility very seriously. A mother's role is extremely special and unique and often has the greatest impact on the lives of her children. It is a role that no other person can replace. A mother's role begins before a baby is conceived. When God is developing the character, values, and principles of a woman, He is also preparing her for her role as a mother—a role in which she will pass down those godly characteristics to her children.

The importance of a mother's role does not diminish as the children grow older. Even when they are grown and have children of their own, the mother continues to be a source of guidance and wisdom. While the role of a mother changes throughout the years, the love, care, nurture, and encouragement given by a mother should never end.

The Gift of Children

Children are an inheritance from the Lord. God is the Creator of all things, and all human life has value because we are made in the image of God. God gives us children through marriage, and the family is created. God made all things, and God owns all things, including children. As parents we sometimes think that our children are our possessions. But we should always remember that our children, along with everything else in this world, belong to God. For a short time, the Lord allows us the privilege of raising these precious children.

The Word of God says, "Behold, children are a heritage from the LORD, the fruit of the womb a reward. Like arrows in the hand of a warrior are the children of one's youth. Blessed is the man who fills his quiver with them! He shall not be put to shame when he speaks with his enemies in the gate" (Psalm 127:3-5, ESV). In these verses, God claims that children are a heritage; another version calls them an inheritance. Elsewhere in Scripture they are called a reward. What powerful words: *heritage, inheritance, reward!* How careful we must be with these precious little ones.

Jesus Himself said, "Whoever receives one such child in my name receives me, but whoever causes one of these little ones who believe in me to sin, it would be better for him to have a great millstone fastened around his neck and to be drowned in the depth of the sea" (Matthew 18:5-6, ESV). He also said, "See that you do not despise one of these little ones. For I tell you that in heaven their angels always see the face of my Father who is in heaven" (Matthew 18:10, ESV). Furthermore, "Fathers, do not provoke your children to anger, but bring them up in the discipline and instruction of the Lord" (Ephesians 6:4, ESV). The Lord gives us these commands because He is the Creator and owner of these children, and He's telling us how we are to provide for them while they are in our care.

Parents have no right or authority to abuse their children—physically, emotionally, or sexually. We must not treat them as slaves or as property. Each of them was made in the image of God, and Christ died for their sins just as He died for ours. The greatest treasures we can leave behind when the Lord calls us home are children who have been well protected, well loved, and well trained, children who are ready to carry the banner of Christ to the next generation.

As parents we are first and foremost called to protect our children: to protect their lives and to protect them from harm or from those who would do them harm. Abortionists are the number one enemy of unborn children. They make their living by taking away the lives of children. The Bible says, "Rescue those being led . . . toward slaughter" (Proverbs 24:11). *Slaughter* is exactly what is in store for many preborn babies if Christians don't offer the hope of Jesus Christ to those dealing with an unplanned pregnancy. As mothers and fathers we must stand up, protect, and defend the children—those that the Lord calls a heritage and a reward.

Marriage Under Attack

Around the world, the institution of marriage is under direct attack, one that will most certainly escalate unless the Church takes a bold stand in defense of marriage. Throughout many countries, marriage rates are decreasing as a result of an ongoing societal attack—perpetuated by the media and by cultural progressives who seek to cast off the shackles of a traditional view of marriage and family. This decline in marriage can be seen in the increase of single parents, the number of children born outside of marriage, high divorce rates, and more couples living together. These realities can be seen in virtually every country on Earth, even in Africa.

Satan hates marriage. Marriage was God's idea for the human race right from the very moment that He created Eve. Destroying a Christian marriage is often one of the most effective weapons to weaken the sanctity of marriage and undermine a growing Church, successful ministry, as well as the entire country.

The destruction of marriage is a win-win situation for the enemy because it hurts people and attacks God. As such, Satan is prepared to invest quite a lot of energy and resources into it. For example, same-sex marriages are not the ultimate goal in the fight to redefine marriage, but *another step* in the process to erase the boundaries of what constitutes marriage and family altogether.

A Pew Research Center survey found that young people are much more inclined than their elders to view living together and other "new family forms," such as same-sex marriage, favorably.[2] Like a frog in a kettle of boiling water, the heat of sexual immorality promoted through a pervasive secular media increases gradually, and most of us are unaware of where it is leading us. Sexual sin, starting with heterosexual immorality, has led us on a course that embraces an "anything goes" mentality. First comes a degrading of marriage, then an embracing of heterosexual immorality, then comes the normalization of homosexuality, and finally an attack on any traditional marriage.

The push for the normalization of homosexuality has been extremely successful in many countries and is all-pervasive. The same-sex machine has set its sights on redefining marriage and is openly hostile to traditional marriage between one man and one woman. The well-funded gay agenda is trying to force homosexual, marriage in many countries.

The newest battle is transgenderism, seeking to embrace the idea that men can become women and women can become men, which is, of course, physically impossible. It is an all-out assault on God's standard of male and female. This totally unhinged belief system has taken root in the United States. Male swimmers and runners now often are champions in women's events. Male contestants are now in female beauty pageants.

The attack against marriage includes messages that say:

- Marriage is "old-fashioned."
- Marriage is unnecessary, because sex outside of marriage has become widely accepted.
- Marriage was designed by men to subjugate women.
- Marriage should include men marrying men and women marrying women.
- Divorce should be accepted when a married couple no longer love each other.
- Living together is a good way to find out if you are compatible before getting married.
- Having children while living together is no different from having children within marriage.

As a result:
- The more secular education children receive, the more they reject traditional marriage.
- Less people are getting married than ever before.
- More young people are experimenting with sex prior to marriage.
- Those who do get married are choosing to have fewer children.
- More educated youth are embracing the LGBTQ+ philosophy.

- More children are being raised in single-parent homes.
- Many children are abandoned at a young age and forced to live on the streets.
- Many unplanned pregnancies end in the death of the child through abortion.

Bigamy

The Bible clearly states, "And the two will become one flesh" (Ephesians 5:31). This is very clear in that it does not allow for multiples of marriage partners. While the Bible records various individuals in the Bible who had multiple wives and concubines, God's command for marriage is clearly between one man and one woman. Marriage that includes more than one wife is not God's best for us, and was never His original plan. But God *allowed* it during Old Testament times due to our sinfulness. Bigamy, having more than one wife, has historical roots in Africa that are deeply intertwined with cultural traditions and practices. In many African societies, the practice of bigamy has been prevalent for centuries. This practice often reflects notions of power, wealth, and social status within these communities.

Bigamy is a distortion of God's original design for marriage. The biblical perspective on marriage emphasizes the sacred union between one man and one woman as God's best intention for human relationships. While the Bible does record instances of men having multiple wives, such as King Solomon and many figures in the Old Testament, it is essential to understand that this practice was never God's original plan. Jesus reaffirmed the importance of monogamous marriage, stating,

> "'Haven't you read,' he replied, 'that at the beginning the Creator "made them male and female" and said, "For this reason a man will leave his father and mother and be united to his wife, and the two will become one flesh?" So they are

no longer two, but one flesh. Therefore what God has joined together, let no one separate.'" (Matthew 19:4-6)

Bigamy diminishes and demeans women by undermining the sacredness of marriage and perpetuating inequality within relationships. It can lead to issues such as neglect, jealousy, and emotional turmoil for all parties involved, especially the woman who may find herself in a position of lesser value or authority within marriage.

Bigamy in Africa, and elsewhere, challenges the foundational principles of Christian marriage by deviating from God's intended design. By embracing the biblical perspective of marriage as a sacred union between one man and one woman, we can honor the sanctity of relationships, promote equality, and uphold the values of love, respect, and commitment within the institution of marriage.

Divorce

The Word of God tells us:

- Marriage is sacred.
- God hates divorce.

Divorce is a reality that happens for many different reasons, but divorce was never God's plan for a husband and wife. A couple should always enter into marriage realizing the holiness of the covenant of marriage and that they have made a vow, a promise, before God to honor, love, and cherish each other as long as they both shall live. Some divorces have biblical authority, some do not, and some men and women are divorced by their spouses through no fault of their own. Perhaps because of the strength of verses like 'For I hate divorce,' says the LORD" (Malachi 2:16, NASB), divorced people are sometimes mistreated in Christian churches.

While the Bible is indeed clear on how the Lord feels about divorce—He hates divorce—the Bible is equally clear on how we should treat one another. Jesus put it best when He said, "Why do you look at the speck of sawdust in your brother's eye and pay no attention to the plank in your own eye?" (Matthew 7:3). All of us have sinned (Romans 3:23), none of us is righteous (Romans 3:10), and we should never fail to extend grace and compassion to all of our Christian brothers and sisters, including the divorced ones.

Gay Marriage

The Bible is clear in stating that marriage is between one man and one woman and is equally clear in condemning the practice of homosexuality. "You shall not lie with a male as with a woman; it is an abomination" (Leviticus 18:22, ESV). The world would have us believe that all love is equal and that a man loving a man is no different from a man loving a woman. Either the Bible is true and is the Word of God or we have been teaching incorrectly for the last 2,000 years, and Jews for the last 4,000 to 6,000 years.

The biblical teaching that marriage is a sacred sacrament between one man and one woman is clearly stated. What is God-ordained cannot be adjusted to suit liberal views. Marriage is heterosexual and monogamous and should be open to the possibility of children. The Bible backs all of this up—sex outside of marriage is a sin—and that is as true for heterosexuals as it is for homosexuals. But the Bible explicitly condemns homosexuality.

There are those who would state that we must be inclusive and love everyone regardless of their behavior. That is true. We love everyone. But that doesn't mean we are forced to approve ungodly behavior. The idea of being inclusive is trying to force us to appear good rather than to be good. The Church should absolutely be inclusive. Christ spent time with tax collectors and prostitutes, but it is they who went away changed, not Christ. We are fallen, therefore we are all sinners. The

Church is open to sinners; that's the purpose of the Church. But it should not encourage people to continue to sin.

Conclusion

Marriage is an institution created by God through which He blesses the world. It is the foundation for all successful societies. The institution of marriage—one man and one woman united before God for life—is under attack by Satan, and the Church must be bold in standing strong for biblical marriage. That same Pew survey that said young people are open to the idea of redefining marriage does have some encouraging news—the vast majority of adults still consider their own family to be the most important, most satisfying element of their lives.[3] May we, with a loving and gracious spirit, continue to uphold and model God's standards of marriage and family.

Chapter 6:
Be Fruitful: The Divine Call to Multiply

I was enjoying my job as a journalist with a promising career in the media industry when the Lord called me into full-time Christian ministry. At the time, I was still a young man in my twenties and was dating a girl. Unfortunately, though we both knew the Lord, we got involved sexually, and she became pregnant. Halfway into her pregnancy, I resigned from my job to serve in ministry with a call to train pastors in Africa. We went before God, repented for our sin, but agreed to keep the pregnancy.

Somehow God blessed my ministry so much, and in a few months I was moving from country to country with great reception among pastors where I taught on disciple-making among oral cultures and other subjects. When my son, Nathaniel, was born, his mother and I began to co-parent.

Coming from a culture of shame, I was always ashamed to talk about my son to the pastors I was mobilizing and training. This was Africa. How do you explain being single, having a son out of wedlock, and leading a ministry? This created a constant feeling of fear and condemnation.

One day while traveling to speak at a Christian missions conference in Hong Kong for a global ministry, I happened to go to a toy store with Pastor Edward Mwansa from Zambia who was a pro-life champion already. Edward was buying toys for his children, and I saw one toy that I figured would be so nice to bring home to my son. Then the thoughts started running in my head, *If I buy the toy, this African pastor will probably ask me who I'm buying it for, and I may be forced to lie that it is for a nephew. I was in a tough spot.* Anyway, I picked up the toy and went straight to the cashier to pay. As soon as I placed it at the cashier's counter, I felt Edward's hand on my shoulder, and he asked, "Who are you buying that nice toy for?" I said, "Edward, let me pay, then we can go outside and talk."

We walked outside and found a bench to speak heart to heart. I told Edward my story and that of my son. I expected him to be shocked, to look at me with condemnation, and then to cause people to close ministry doors for me because of this. But Edward instead told me his own story of the miscarriages they had encountered with his wife, her past abortions, and the shame she had overcome to lead an international pro-life ministry. He then gave me a good hug, led me in a prayer of embracing God's forgiveness, and encouraged me that my son preciously bears the image of God regardless of the circumstances surrounding his conception. My life changed forever from that moment on a bench in a distant city away from Africa. Then Edward told me something: "Abortion is real in Africa. The message of the sacredness of human life is desperately needed in the continent. It is pastors like you and me that will make a difference by doing the uncomfortable job of coming out with our stories to pave a way for the message of life through the Church in Africa."

The following year at a pastors prayer conference that I was leading in Kenya, I told sixty-five pastors my story. Then I invited any who had been involved with abortion or similarly had had children out of wedlock to come forward for repentance, forgiveness, and healing. Half the room came forward. One bishop said to me *with tears in his eyes, "I have a child outside my marriage that I have never been able to tell my wife about. The mother of the child threatens to destroy my family and ministry, saying she will bring the child to church and make a public disgrace of me. So I keep taking God's money from the church to bribe her to be quiet." After prayer, he and his wife talked about it, and his wife helped him to reach out to the other woman saying, "It's okay, we want to help raise the child. He is innocent and is made in the image of God, and he deserves to know his father." The bishop and his wife have since gone on to become great pro-life ministers in their region.*

This experience tells me that the Church in Africa is a sleeping giant when it comes to pro-life ministry. When Church leaders embrace the truth of the sacredness of human life, they influence whole communities to become life-giving as a cultural norm.

Bramuel Musya
Mission Mobilizer, Via Africa Life Coordinator
Life Equip Global

Sex and the Bible

Bramuel's story underlines the powerful truth that God created sex as the means for creating children in a marriage relationship. When we engage in sex outside of marriage, we violate God's law and open the door for a number of problems. But Bramuel's story also highlights the powerful truth that God is a merciful and redeeming Father.

We are in the middle of the greatest war of all time. It is a war waged by Satan and his demons against God and His children. And one of Satan's greatest tools in this war is attacking us in regard to sex. This is not to say that sex is the problem. Quite the contrary, sex is one of God's greatest gifts to us—and one we have never fully understood in terms of the fullness of the richness it provides in understanding

God's love. No, the problem is how we have allowed Satan to corrupt human sexuality for selfish and sinful purposes.

Author and spiritual teacher Ronald Rolheiser said, "Sex is not just like anything else, despite our culture's protest. Its fire is so powerful, so precious, so close to the heart and soul of a person, and so godly, that it either gives life or it takes it away. It can never be casual, but is either a sacrament or a destructive act."[1]

Sex is one of the most difficult subjects for Christians to talk about. Christians are often too ashamed or embarrassed to talk about sex. But this attitude doesn't come from God. In fact there are 119 verses in the Bible that refer to sex. And an entire book of the Bible—Song of Songs—explores the theme of love and intimacy within the context of a committed relationship. It depicts the beauty and sanctity of romantic love, marriage, and sexual desire in a respectful manner.

Song of Songs celebrates the physical and emotional connection between a husband and wife, emphasizing the importance of mutual respect, devotion, and fidelity. Through poetic and metaphorical language, Song of Songs portrays sexuality as a gift from God, highlighting the significance of honoring one's partner within the boundaries of a loving and committed relationship. While our sexuality is a gift from the Lord, sexual behavior of *any* kind is forbidden outside of marriage—and for good reason. It harms us spiritually, emotionally, and sometimes physically. It is a grave sin against God.

Why must we even talk about sex? Because sex outside of marriage is responsible for the following:

- One hundred twenty-one million pregnancies occur every year due to sex outside of marriage.[2]
- Seventy-three million babies are killed by abortion every year.[3]
- There are 376 million new cases of STDs and STIs worldwide every year.[4]

- One in three women worldwide experiences sexual violence, including rape and incest.[5]
- One hundred million mothers raise children without a husband.[6]
- It is estimated that there are over five million sex slaves globally.[7]

Globally, marriage rates are declining, while divorces are increasing. Sexual trafficking is at an all-time high. Homosexuality is growing exponentially. The pornography industry has addicted hundreds of millions of men and women and generates over $97 billion in revenue around the world annually.[8]

Be Fruitful and Multiply

The Bible tells us to "Be fruitful and multiply" (Genesis 1:28, ESV). In order to fulfill this command, He has given us marriage and sex. Children are to be received as an expression of God's goodness and grace, not as a curse or an inconvenience. But while God encourages the creation of children, and repeatedly states that having many children is a result of His blessing, Satan is encouraging men and women to have fewer and fewer children, or to have no children at all. Satan wants us to be sterile through birth control and kill the children we have through abortion. He does this through the culture which he influences.

God's creation of a human being through the sexual union of two people is a miracle. At the exact moment of conception, a unique human being—body, soul, and spirit—comes into existence. Never before has one existed and never again will another exist.

The first part of the creation mandate commands us to "Be fruitful and multiply." In other words, God wants families to grow. He wants more people to share in His fellowship. The Bible does not instruct married couples on how many children to have, but it does state that children are a blessing. Unfortunately, many cultures see population increase as a burden, not a blessing. Birth rates in many countries are below "replacement rate." Seeing babies as unwanted is the result of a fallen culture. We, as Christians, should see babies as blessings.

God had just finished all His creation, ending with His masterpieces, the very first man and woman. The world was now fully created with days and nights, seasons and years, plants and animals, and Adam and Eve. God set His plan in motion to fill the world He created with people (Isaiah 45:18). The world was Adam and Eve's inheritance to fill, and as stated in the beginning of Genesis 1:28, it was God's blessing for Adam and Eve to have children and work the earth.

Simply put, God desired for Adam and Eve to have many children and for their children to have many children. Satan wants to thwart God's plan by getting people not to marry, to become homosexual or transsexual, to embrace birth control, or to kill the babies they create through abortion. All of these options prevent the multiplication of life—and lead to physical and spiritual death.

Satan wants humanity to use artificial birth control so we don't conceive children, and if that fails, he will try to get people to kill the baby they have conceived through abortion. The word *contraception* comes from the Latin words "against" and "conception"—essentially "against pregnancy." Contraception is any method, device, or drug used for the purpose of preventing a baby from being conceived as a result of sexual intercourse. The name itself, "against conception," tells us it is against what God intends—that we "be fruitful and multiply."

Pregnancy is God's natural and intended consequence for sexual intercourse. Artificial birth control methods are an attempt to prevent with drugs or other devices what God created the body to do naturally. All chemical contraceptives—including The Pill—have the potential of acting as an abortifacient—that is, ending the life of the child after it is conceived. The use of artificial birth control and contraceptives puts us in the mindset that sexual intercourse is merely for recreation and that the creation of a child is an accident that must be avoided at all costs. The world encourages sex and discourages children. Birth control is how Satan entices people to engage in sex without creating new life.

When couples rely on birth control and it fails—as it sometimes does—then they often fall back on abortion. The act of sexual intercourse is a sacred act, reserved for marriage because of the potential of creating human life. As such, it is important that we realize that it is God who opens and closes the womb. Is God sovereign over all creation but somehow absent when a child is being conceived? No! God is *always* sovereign!

What does the Bible say about God creating life?

> Behold, children are a heritage from the LORD, the fruit of the womb a reward. (Psalm 127:3, ESV)

> Your wife will be like a fruitful vine within your house; your children will be like olive shoots around your table. (Psalm 128:3, ESV)

> Your offspring shall be like the dust of the earth, and you shall spread abroad to the west and to the east and to the north and to the south, and in you and your offspring shall all the families of the earth be blessed. (Genesis 28:14, ESV)

Sex and Marriage

The Bible tells us that in the beginning, after God created the heavens and the earth, after God created the first man, God took a rib from Adam's side while he slept and fashioned it into a woman, whom He named Eve. God presented Eve to Adam, and their union was sanctified by the Lord. He blessed them and said, "Be fruitful and multiply and fill the earth and subdue it" (Genesis 1:28, ESV). In this act, God established the institution of marriage and commanded humanity to embrace the multiplication of life by having children through sex.

When we choose to engage in sexual activity as God ordained it—within marriage—then it is a life-giving act, a holy act. When a fire is in its proper place—such as a fireplace or firepit—it provides many helpful benefits. We can cook over the fire. The fire provides heat and light. The fire is pleasant to look at. But when a fire is not in its proper place, it becomes all consuming, destroying everything in its path. Sex is like that. When we choose to engage in sex outside of God's boundaries, it becomes a destructive fire.

The Bible says, "Let marriage be held in honor among all, and let the marriage bed be undefiled, for God will judge the sexually immoral and adulterous" (Hebrews 13:4, ESV).

Only when two people are married are they free to know each other completely and sexually, and as a result receive the blessing of children who would fill the Earth. The choice of sex is just that: a choice. And the church must teach that that choice must be reserved for marriage. We must also teach that that choice may lead to the conception of a child. And that we must *never* end the life of that child through abortion.

We all have a sexual drive. When our sexual drive is properly channeled in marriage, women and men can be cocreators of life, offering protection and being champions of life. But when men are not properly taught to respect and protect their sexuality until marriage, they can become predators, ravenously taking whatever they desire. This is why it is so important that the Church teaches about biblical sexuality.

Sexual Immorality

What is sexual immorality? In the New Testament, the word most often translated as "sexual immorality" is *porneia*, which also means "whoredom, fornication, and idolatry." Sexual immorality involves any type of sexual expression or behavior outside the boundaries of a biblically defined marriage relationship. In 1 Peter 1:16 we read, "Be holy, because I am holy." We are made in His image, and we should reflect God in everything we do. That means we should abstain from all sin, especially sexual immorality.

Satan uses the media, movies, the music industry, and many organizations such as Planned Parenthood that directly oppose God's Word regarding sexuality and life to spread immoral sexual behavior to every corner of the world. The consequences of sexual immorality include wounded hearts, sexual addictions, adultery, masturbation, depression, STIs, suicides, rapes, sexual trafficking, sexual abuse, prostitution, pornography, sadomasochism, divorce, an avalanche of unwanted pregnancies, and tens of millions of preborn children being killed every year by abortion.

All over the world, every aspect of our life is impacted by our media-saturated culture, and it's only getting worse. Media and sex go hand in hand. Everything—from the phones and computers we use to communicate, to the movies and TV shows we watch, to the clothes we wear and the sports we cheer for—they are all soaked in unbiblical sexuality. Sex is used to entice, provoke, hook, and sell us.

What does the Bible say about sexual immorality? Paul, inspired by the Holy Spirit, said in Corinth.

> You know that wicked people will not inherit the kingdom of God, don't you? Stop deceiving yourselves! Sexually immoral people, idolaters, adulterers, male prostitutes, homosexuals, thieves, greedy people, drunks, slanderers, and robbers will not inherit the kingdom of God. (1 Corinthians 6:9-10, isv)

> Flee from sexual immorality. All other sins a person commits are outside the body, but whoever sins sexually, sins against their own body. (1 Corinthians 6:18)

> Put to death, therefore, whatever belongs to your earthly nature: sexual immorality, impurity, lust, evil desires and greed, which is idolatry. (Colossians 3:5)

> It is God's will that you should be sanctified: that you should avoid sexual immorality; that each of you should learn to control your own body in a way that is holy and honorable, not in passionate lust like the pagans, who do not know God. (1 Thessalonians 4:3-5)

It's difficult to find any issue that has had a more harmful impact on the lives of individuals, families, the Church, and the community than sexual immorality. The resulting heartbreak of emotional wounds, the destruction caused by sexual addictions, the confusion of homosexuality and gender identity issues, the disaster of unwanted pregnancies, and the devastation of the killing of innocent children by abortion are immeasurable.

The battle for sexual purity is one of the toughest battles in both the physical and the spiritual realm. This is especially true in modern times because the culture of the "sexual revolution" has made sex into an idol, a false god, that is to be worshiped at the expense of the human being and of love.

Few areas of our life make us feel as disqualified to serve God as the condemnation, confusion, and bondage that come from violating our relationship with God through sexual sins. The truth is that there are no unwounded warriors in this battle. Whether from past sexual sins committed by us or against us, selfishness or disobedience, or any of a hundred acts of rebellion, we all have been wounded in one way or another.

The wonderful news, the great news, is that while we may be wounded, we are not worthless! You may have been involved in premarital sex, had an abortion, been raped, or have a sexual addiction. You may have been the abuser or been abused. Still the Word of God tells us that through repentance we can receive God's unmerited forgiveness.

Through His death on the cross, Jesus the Messiah, the Son of God, the spotless sacrificial lamb, has paid a price once and for all that ensures our forgiveness and restoration. Our pardon, our forgiveness, is complete and without limitations—and too wonderful to understand. Christ's saving work on the cross has established our complete redemption. Regardless of what occurred in your past, your future is full of promise! Through repentance and forgiveness, you are a 100 percent qualified first-line representative of Jesus Christ to our world.

Don't let Satan's lies rob you of your birthright. You are a child of God in full standing!

Teaching About Sex

Restoring a biblical understanding of human sexuality will go a long way toward decreasing sexual immorality, divorce, STIs (HIV/AIDS), sexual abuse, sexual trafficking, rape, incest, unplanned pregnancies, and abortions. The Church of Jesus Christ needs to value and teach about the sanctity of human life and biblical human sexuality. As they communicate the teachings of the Bible with such clarity and so infused with the power of the Holy Spirit, the Church becomes a true place of education, hope, refuge, and healing in matters related to sex.

Where the Church has *not* spoken powerfully regarding the Bible's stance on sexual issues and what is true biblical sexuality, Satan has spread his lies, corruption, and perversion. As followers of Christ we must respond—first in our own lives, then in the lives of our spouses, children, and family—with sound biblical teaching, extending outward until we are a true blessing to our community, encouraging life-affirming behaviors and decisions. Christians all around the world are having abortions because they have believed Satan's lies about babies in the womb. The Church *must* respond with Bible-based, truthful, and medically accurate teaching.

One of the roles of the Church is to teach the entire Word of God. When the Church does not teach about the sanctity of human life and God's standards on sexuality, we default to whatever is our culture's standard on sexuality. The Bible is *the* textbook on life and human sexuality. It sets standards and expectations. We need to teach God's plan for sexuality to all believers. Satan has worked at corrupting that gift from the beginning. He has used the corruption of sexuality to harm great numbers of men, women, and children in the body of Christ and throughout the world. The Church must respond with sound biblical teaching that equips, educates, and prepares the members of the body for Satan's attack.

Western Influence

Globalization has brought about the widespread distribution of Western movies, music, TV shows, and the internet to various parts of the world, including Africa. While these cultural exchanges have had some positive outcomes, it is crucial to acknowledge the many negative impacts they have had, particularly on African children. Western influences have contributed greatly to an increase in sexual immorality among African youth, leading to a surge in unplanned pregnancies, abortions, sexually transmitted diseases (STDs), and maternal mortality rates.

Sexualization in Western Media
Western media often portrays explicit sexual content, including music with provocative or pornographic lyrics, videos, movies, and TV shows. African children who are exposed to such content at a young age are susceptible to distorted perceptions of relationships, sexuality, and gender roles.

Influence of Internet and Social Media
The internet, with its vast Western platforms, has become a double-edged sword. While it offers valuable educational resources, it also exposes African children to explicit content and pornographic material. These harmful influences are contributing to premature sexual exploration and risky behaviors.

Impact on Sexual Behavior
The exposure to Western media has been linked to an increase in sexual promiscuity among African youth. Studies have shown that the prevalence of sex outside of marriage has risen significantly in countries such as South Africa, Nigeria, and Kenya. This shift in behavior has led to a surge in STDs, including HIV/AIDS, gonorrhea, and syphilis as well as pregnancies and abortions.

Unplanned Pregnancies and Abortions
The rise in sexual immorality has resulted in a parallel increase in unplanned pregnancies across Africa. Countries like Zimbabwe, Uganda, and Ghana have seen alarming rates of teenage pregnancies, often leading to increased abortions and maternal mortality.

Western influences, ranging from movies and music to the internet and TV shows, have had a negative impact on African children, contributing to an increase in sexual immorality and its consequences. To address these challenges, it is crucial for the African Church to address these issues frankly, accurately, and biblically. By doing so, we can empower African youth to make healthy Christ-honoring decisions and navigate the complexities of a globalized world while preserving purity, their health, and cultural values.

Conclusion

As Christian defenders of life, let's encourage the Christian community to be bold in defending the sanctity of human life and promoting the biblical use of sexuality within marriage in a way that brings life and not death. Restoring a biblical understanding of human sexuality will go a long way toward decreasing sexual immorality, unplanned pregnancies, and abortions. The Church of Jesus Christ needs to value and teach about the sanctity of human life and biblical human sexuality and communicate the teachings of the Bible with such clarity and so infused with the power of the Holy Spirit that the Church becomes a true place of education, hope, refuge, and healing in matters related to sex.

Chapter 7:
Choices and Consequences:
The Hidden Realities of Abortion Methods

Many women hide the secret of abortion deep in their hearts, and they are suffering severe consequences. I was one of those women. When, as a twenty-three-year-old, I chose to end my pregnancy, I was clueless about what God had to say about abortion. To be honest, I didn't know what God had to say about much of anything. As a college student, I had fought for a woman's "right to a safe and legal abortion." I wrote papers, signed petitions, and argued the pro-choice stance. It all seemed so enlightened at the time—until the day that choice was mine. In that moment of free choice, my only guiding emotions were shame, despair, and fear.

For a few extra dollars, my doctor arranged for me to sleep through my routine procedure at a local hospital. My plan was to have the abortion and never look back. I still remember struggling to wake up after having an allergic reaction to the anesthesia. I labored for breath through a respirator. I also remember the pained expressions on the faces of my mom and dad as they stood by my bed in the emergency room. The blanketing silence that fell in those moments lasted for the next seven years.

God says, "Today I have given you the choice between life and death, between blessings and curses. Now I call on heaven and earth to witness the choice you make. Oh, that you would choose

> life!" (Deuteronomy 30:19, NLT). God's Word and His truth began to fill all of the empty places in my heart and my life. But this was not an easy process. It was a time of allowing God into the darkest secrets of my past to reveal all of my sin and brokenness in exchange for redemption and purpose. What an awesome exchange it was!
>
> As God's Word and God's people began to show me the way to healing and wholeness, I began to ask God to use me and my story to reach other women. In 1986, God gave birth to a ministry that serves as a Christian alternative to abortion called *A Woman's Place Ministries*. After ministering to so many women who have endured the heartbreak of abortion, God led me to write a post-abortion recovery Bible study/video called *Surrendering the Secret*, which provides a path to healing and restoration for those who have been trapped by the abortion lie, as I was. God says in Isaiah that He desires to turn ashes into beauty (Isaiah 61:3). My life is a reflection of that promise.
>
> Pat Layton
President and Founder
Surrendering the Secret

The Reality of Abortion

In many countries, including many in Africa, babies in the womb are not considered persons, are not protected by law, and can be killed for little or no reason at all. In every country on Earth, preborn babies are being killed either through surgical or chemical abortions or traditional means including poisoning, being left to die, and infanticide (killing the baby immediately after it is born). But exactly what is abortion?

- Abortion is Satan's lie that we should kill our children.
- Abortion is Satan's lie that killing our children is our right.

- Abortion is Satan's lie that killing our children sets us free economically.
- Abortion is Satan's lie!

Abortion is the intentional killing of an innocent child, who is made in the image of God, while still in its mother's womb. In an unplanned or unwanted pregnancy, a woman has three options: carry the pregnancy to term and parent the baby, carry the pregnancy to term and make an adoption decision for the baby, or end the life of the baby through abortion. Often pressured by the father of the child, family, or even the Church, the woman in an unplanned pregnancy might consider an abortion as the least traumatizing of all options. It may be seen as the "quick fix" to a problem. Even someone that knows the truth and has a strong faith in God may lean toward abortion believing, "God will forgive me." This is a horrible misunderstanding of God's grace. We should *never* take the grace of God for granted.

Abortion always involves killing an innocent life—destroying the life of a developing baby either through the use of chemicals, by surgically entering the uterus and dismembering and sucking out the baby, or by using traditional methods such as massages or the use of herbs. Abortion is the sacrifice of a human life for our own personal convenience. We insist that our children must die so that we may live the life we want. Abortion is the ultimate act of selfishness.

The truth is, a woman is never the same once she is pregnant, whether the child is kept, adopted, or aborted. Once pregnant, a woman can never be unpregnant. The seeds of an abortion are planted when two people engage in sexual activity without thinking of the potential child they are creating. They forget, or they don't know, or they choose to ignore the fact that sexual activity is more than recreational—sex is a reproductive act.

Doctors will often talk about ending a pregnancy. We must

understand the fact that abortion ends a pregnancy by killing the developing baby. You can never end a pregnancy without ending the life of a growing human baby. Most women who choose abortion, like Pat at the beginning of this chapter, have not been educated about the physical, emotional, psychological, and spiritual damage an abortion does to a woman's body and heart. They certainly have not been shown how their baby will be painfully destroyed.

The *choice* of abortion kills a child and often damages the mother. Those who promote abortion often do so because of the profit motive. Planned Parenthood, the world's largest abortion provider, reported $1.9 billion in income from 2021 to 2022. One of the ways pro-abortion organizations have changed the dialogue is to promote abortion as a *choice*—a fundamental women's right, not as a dangerous surgery that ends the life of a child and hurts a woman physically, emotionally, and spiritually. The baby, from the first instant of conception, is a living person made in the image of God—not a *choice*.

The Bible—the ultimate authority for all human life—tells us, "You shall not kill" (Exodus 20:13, NCB); instead we are to *defend* life, especially the life of our own children. Parents are supposed to be willing to die for their children, not the other way around.

Those who promote abortion as a woman's *choice* say that abortion needs to be safe and legal. Any surgery in which a person always loses their life may be legal, but it can never be safe. There is no beneficial effect of abortion on a baby. It always kills a child and potentially damages the mother emotionally and spiritually, if not physically. The *choice* of abortion is humans trying to deal with the situation, thinking they can erase what has happened. Abortion is the result of lack of understanding, lack of knowledge, and lack of knowing the Word of God. Abortion is never a *reset button*. After an abortion, a woman can never be unpregnant. She will always have to live with the truth that she was pregnant and made the *choice* to kill her baby by abortion.

The History of Abortion

The killing of babies by sacrifice and abortion can be traced back to ancient civilizations. Historical evidence suggests that methods such as herbal concoctions, physical manipulation, and sharp objects were used to induce abortion in times past. Shockingly, these methods are still being used today. In biblical times, the practice of killing babies and sacrificing them to idols was widespread. In ancient Greece and Rome, abortion was common. During the Middle Ages, the Christian Church exerted significant influence, and abortion was generally considered a sin.

In the 1800s, laws against abortion began to emerge in different countries, including the United States and European nations. These laws were primarily based on moral and religious grounds, aiming to protect the life of babies in the womb and discourage women from seeking abortions. By the early 1900s, most countries had strict laws prohibiting abortion[1] except in cases where the mother's life was at risk. In the mid-twentieth century we witnessed a revolutionary and evil shift in attitudes toward sexuality, birth control, and abortion.

The Soviet Union played a significant role in modernizing and popularizing abortion as a method of population control. In the 1950s, the Soviet Union implemented policies that allowed for the widespread use of state-sponsored abortion as a means of eliminating unwanted babies.[2] This approach was driven by the communist government's desire to control population growth. As the Soviet Union embraced and promoted abortion, it influenced other developed nations to consider similar measures. The availability and acceptance of abortion as a method of family planning began to multiply throughout the world, particularly in Western countries.

The late twentieth century saw abortions multiplying across the globe. In 1973, the landmark U.S. Supreme Court case Roe v. Wade legalized abortion in the United States throughout all nine months of pregnancy. Other countries, such as Canada and France, followed the lead of the U.S. and liberalized their laws around this time. Today nearly 90 percent of nations worldwide permit abortions for one reason or another, and there are over a dozen countries in the world, like the United States, that allow the killing of babies with no restrictions at all, allowing babies even in the ninth month to be killed.[3]

Types of Abortion

All abortions fall into three categories:

- Chemical
- Surgical
- Traditional

All abortions violate the most basic medical tenet, "Above all, do no harm." In an abortion procedure, one patient always dies. The following information is graphic and extremely disturbing. I encourage you to stop before going forward and prepare yourself in prayer. It is vital for you to know what an abortion is and what you are protecting a woman and her baby from.

D&C Abortion[4]

A first-trimester Dilation and Curettage (D&C) abortion, also known as a suction abortion, is a medical procedure used to take the life of a baby within the first twelve weeks. It is the most common *surgical* abortion.

1. Preparation: Before the procedure, the woman may undergo a medical evaluation, including a physical examination, blood tests, and if needed an ultrasound to confirm the age of the baby.
2. Anesthesia: She may be given local anesthesia, conscious sedation, or general anesthesia.

3. Dilating the Cervix: The person doing the abortion will use a speculum. This is a device to open the vaginal canal to gain access to the cervix. The cervix is the lower, narrow end of the uterus that forms a canal between the uterus and vagina. Dilators, or steel metal rods, will then be used to open or dilate the cervix.
4. Uterine Aspiration: Once the cervix is sufficiently dilated, a thin tube called a cannula is inserted into the uterus. The cannula is connected to a suction device, such as a manual or electric vacuum aspiration system. The vacuum aspirator is ten to twenty times more powerful than a home vacuum cleaner. The abortionist uses suction to tear the baby into pieces and suck it out of the mother's womb. The baby, now in pieces, is sucked into the suction machine followed by the placenta.
5. Curettage: After the aspiration, a curette, which is a sharp instrument shaped like a long spoon, is used to scrape the uterine lining to ensure the complete removal of the baby and the placenta.
6. Examination and Recovery: The abortionist examines all the pieces of the baby—legs, arms, hands, feet, torso, and head—to make sure the baby has been totally removed. If anything is missing, he must scrape her uterus again.

D&E Abortion[5]

A baby is considerably larger in the second trimester, anywhere from three inches in the fourth month to as large as nine inches in the sixth month. For that reason, a suction abortion will not work on a baby that size, and a different procedure is needed. This *surgical* procedure is called Dilation and Evacuation (D&E).

1. To prepare for a D&E abortion, the abortionist uses laminaria, a form of sterilized seaweed, to open the woman's cervix twenty-four to forty-eight hours before the procedure. The laminaria

soaks up liquid from the woman's body and expands, widening or dilating the cervix.

2. When the woman returns to the abortion clinic, the abortionist may administer anesthesia and further open the cervix using metal dilators and a speculum. The abortionist inserts a large suction catheter into the uterus and turns it on, emptying the amniotic fluid.

3. After the amniotic fluid is removed, the abortionist uses a sopher clamp—a grasping instrument with rows of sharp teeth—to grasp and pull the baby's arms and legs, tearing the limbs from the child's body. The abortionist continues to grasp intestines, spine, heart, lungs, and any other limbs or body parts. The most difficult part of the procedure is usually finding, grasping, and crushing the baby's head. After removing pieces of the child's skull, the abortionist uses a curette to scrape the uterus and remove the placenta and any remaining parts of the baby. The abortionist then collects all of the baby's parts and reassembles them to make sure there are two arms, two legs, and that all of the pieces have been removed. Most women feel some pain during the procedure.

4. After a D&E abortion, the woman will be given a pad to help with the bleeding and will usually be sent to a recovery room where she will sit with other women who have had abortions. It is not unusual for there to be significant crying from the women who have experienced a painful surgery and the loss of their babies. Many women who have had abortions report having felt high levels of pain, some in spite of receiving anesthesia.

Medical (Chemical) Abortion Procedures

Chemical abortions, like surgical abortions, end the life of the baby in the uterus. Two examples of *chemical* abortions are the abortion pill and the morning after pill (Plan B).

The Abortion Pill[6]

"Abortion Pill" is the common name for using two different drugs to end the life of a developing baby. A baby needs a hormone called progesterone to grow normally. Mifepristone (also called RU-486) blocks the body's own progesterone, stopping the baby from growing and killing the baby. Then a second drug, misoprostol, is taken either right away or up to forty-eight hours later. This drug causes labor, cramping, and bleeding, and the dead baby and uterine lining are expelled from the body. The woman is then sent home to deliver her dead baby. The second pill taken during the Abortion Pill process begins labor contractions in order to expel the baby and uterine lining. This process can take a number of hours, and because contractions similar to those during labor are occurring, it is usually quite painful. Chemical abortions are supposed to be done for up to ten weeks of development. But women often take them at a later date, which makes it much more dangerous for the woman.

The Morning-After Pill (Plan B)[7]

Plan B is considered an emergency contraceptive which can be taken up to seventy-two hours after unprotected sex. The Plan B website promises that "Plan B is not the Abortion Pill" and "Plan B will not terminate an existing pregnancy." This may sound good until you read what else the product information says.

The main ingredient of Plan B is the steroid levonorgestrel. Its product information states that it works by "preventing the release of an egg from the ovary or preventing fertilization of the egg by sperm (male reproductive cells)." It also may work by "changing the lining of the uterus (womb) to prevent development of a pregnancy." That means it would kill a developing baby by not allowing it to implant in its mother's womb.

Implantation always involves an already conceived person—at a tiny level of development. So anything that prevents that tiny baby from implanting itself into the uterus is actually an abortifacient—which is a drug that causes an abortion.

The problem with the morning-after pill is that a woman cannot be sure of how it works. It may have prevented a pregnancy by preventing ovulation, or it may have prevented a tiny baby from implanting in the uterus, which is causing an abortion.[8] Another problem with the morning-after pill is that women may take these hormones and not really actually be pregnant. Later, when they find out how these hormones can cause an abortion, they may feel guilty that they caused an abortion when they were not actually pregnant. The enemy of our souls will do anything to cause guilt and shame.

In some countries these chemicals can now be sold over the internet without any medical supervision. If taken too far along in pregnancy, they might not work and can cause bleeding and danger to the mother. If the pregnancy is an ectopic pregnancy (the baby is stuck in the fallopian tube) and the abortion pills are taken, the ectopic pregnancy can remain undiagnosed and be life-threatening. More and more abortions are and will be chemical abortions.[9] A woman doing this on her own might cause physical and emotional harm to herself. A great danger in any abortion is possible Rh sensitization. If a woman has a negative blood type and the baby has a positive blood type, the mother will make antibodies against Rh-positive blood. In this instance, RhoGAM needs to be given to prevent the antibody formation. Women who have home chemical abortions will not receive RhoGAM. This could cause problems for future pregnancies.

Traditional Abortion Methods

In Africa, traditional abortion methods have been practiced for centuries. These traditional methods vary across different regions and communities on the continent but are more common the further away you get from large cities. Some common traditional abortion techniques in Africa include:

1. Herbal Remedies: Herbal concoctions made from local plants and herbs are ingested or inserted into the vagina to induce abortion.[10] These remedies are often administered without proper dosage or supervision, leading to severe complications.
2. Physical Trauma: Some women resort to physical trauma such as inserting sharp objects into the uterus or using excessive force to induce abortion, which can cause internal injuries and infections.[11]
3. Hot Water Douching: This method involves using hot water or other substances to wash out the uterus, which can lead to burns, infections, and other serious health issues.[12]

The dangerous side effects of these traditional abortion techniques in Africa include:

1. Severe Infections: Improperly administered abortions can lead to serious infections in the reproductive organs, which may result in sepsis or long-term health complications.[13]
2. Hemorrhage: Excessive bleeding is a common risk associated with traditional abortion methods, which can lead to anemia, shock, and even death if not treated promptly.[14]
3. Uterine Perforation: Inserting objects into the uterus or using forceful methods can cause perforation or damage to the uterine wall, leading to internal bleeding and the need for emergency medical intervention.[15]
4. Infertility: Complications from traditional abortions can result in scarring of the reproductive organs, increasing the risk of infertility and future pregnancy complications.[16]
5. Mental Health Issues: Women who undergo traditional abortions may experience guilt, trauma, and psychological distress, impacting their mental well-being and overall quality of life.[17]

6. Death: Traditional abortions, as well as modern abortions, always bring the possibility of severe injury, hemorrhaging, or infection, leading to death.[18]

Does a Baby in the Womb Feel Pain?

Scientific research has shed light on the development of the nervous system in the preborn baby, helping us understand when and how a baby in the womb feels pain. A baby's pain receptors begin to develop at four weeks, followed by nerve fibers that carry messages to the brain. At six weeks, the baby will respond to touch. At eight weeks, the cerebral cortex starts to develop and will eventually grow to have the same number of nerves as an adult. If a baby is touched at ten weeks, his or her hands and eyes will open and close. Not only can the baby smile at twelve weeks, he or she now swallows and responds to simple stimulation of the skin. By twelve weeks, all physiological connections are in place to feel pain.

Many scientists believe that by the fifteenth week of gestation, the neural pathways necessary for pain perception are established.[19] The presence of specialized nerve fibers, known as nociceptors, further suggests the ability of the baby to feel pain.

When considering abortion procedures, especially those performed surgically as the baby grows, the potential for the preborn baby to experience pain becomes a critical issue. Methods such as dilation and evacuation (D&E), which involves dismembering the baby, must make us ask the question—how could we possibly torture a developing baby in this manner?

Dr. Paul Ranalli is a neurologist, lecturer, and clinical instructor at the University of Toronto Medical School. He is also an active researcher, frequent writer on life issues, and an advisory board member for the deVeber Institute for Bioethics and Social Research. In a presentation he gave in October 2008 in Toronto on the topic of

"A Medical Detective Story: What You Felt Before You Were Born," Dr. Ranalli stated, "The fetal brain has the full complement of brain cells present in adulthood, ready and waiting to receive pain signals from the body, and their electrical activity can be recorded by standard electroencephalography."[20]

Why Abortion?

What drives an abortion choice? Why would a woman make the *choice* of abortion? Often because they are being forced to. Sometimes out of ignorance, anger, rebellion, foolishness, or lack of knowledge. Sometimes people are enslaved or addicted to sin. Sometimes it is merely willful disobedience. It is important that we take the time to consider the reasons, circumstances, thoughts, emotions, and pressures—as well as the risk factors—that drive an abortion decision. These risk factors may drive the woman to believe that an abortion may be her best option to preserve her sense of well-being.

Risk factors for abortion include:

- Men abandoning or forcing them
- Poverty
- Lack of knowledge, wisdom, or understanding

Many women who have abortions do so because of a combination of lack of support or pressure from the father of the baby or her family, pressure from culture or medical individuals, worldly deceptions, wrong beliefs, and lack of knowledge. They feel pressured, abandoned, hopeless, and scared. Most women who have an abortion feel they have no other choice.

This is why understanding God's Word regarding the sanctity of human life and intervening in her life is so critical. By understanding what is driving her toward an abortion, we can be better equipped to release the pressure that is affecting that decision. We can provide the hope she craves. We can provide the knowledge she needs. And we can provide the love of Christ, which provides life. You are not just an advocate for the baby in the womb. You are also an advocate for the mother carrying that baby.

When speaking with a woman that is considering an abortion, remember that you are an ambassador of Christ. You don't just represent yourself. You represent Jesus, the King of Kings! When Jesus spoke to the woman caught in adultery, He did not condemn her. He helped her. We must do the same. It is Satan who accuses, not us. Our job is to defend life. First, we must make a connection with the woman. Make sure you are speaking to her out of love. Seek to understand what is driving her to consider having an abortion.

Use the five smooth stones we talked about earlier.

1. Love—Demonstrate the love of God to her by showing her love, mercy, and compassion.
2. Truth—Help her understand the truth of being a mother, that she is carrying a baby, that the baby is alive, and that abortion is the killing of that innocent baby. Tell her about God and Jesus who love her and are ready to come beside her.
3. Knowledge—She is probably unaware of the reality of the child growing inside her. Teach her about that reality. Educate her about how abortions are done and how an abortion will kill her baby and potentially harm her emotionally, physically, and spiritually.
4. Hope—She may be feeling hopeless. Help her understand that she is not alone. That you are there to help. And that God is very aware of her situation and has sent *you* to help *her*.
5. Courage—Help her to see that she is stronger than she thinks. Hundreds of millions of women have chosen life when abortion

seemed like the easier option. They did it because they had the courage to make an incredibly difficult yet unselfish and life-giving choice. Help her have the courage to choose life.

Finally, remember to always speak about the baby, not the pregnancy. Always reinforce the reality that she is already a mother, not just when the baby is born.

What are some of the mother's *internal risk factors* for abortion?
- Does not believe it is morally wrong.
- Does not believe it's a baby or a person.

What are some *external pressures and risk factors* for abortion?
- Life situations: school, work
- Pressure from husband, parents, boyfriend, friends
- Financial issues: poverty can create huge pressure to abort the baby

What kind of fears might she have?
- Her parents/church/others finding out
- Impact on her (or family's) finances
- Fear of raising a child by herself

What might she be confused about?
- The reality of the life of the preborn baby
- Receiving conflicting advice or pressure from others
- Fears like "How can I provide for the child and myself without the help of the father or family?"

The following are some of the major reasons for wanting an abortion as well as some possible responses. These are not intended for you to memorize and quote them to the woman when she has these reasons for an abortion. They are designed to help you understand that there are responses to these reasons, and to help you prepare to respond lovingly, intelligently, and compassionately.

Reason for Abortion #1: "I can't afford a baby."
Potential Responses:
- "Have you ever known anyone that has been single/in your situation and made a decision to parent their baby? How are they doing?"
- Explain that many other women have been in her situation and succeeded, overcoming similar obstacles.
- "Let's discuss what options you have. What are your challenges?"

Reason for Abortion #2: "I'm not ready for a child right now."
Potential Responses:
- Tell her: "The future is yet to come, the baby is here, he or she exists." Abortion may seem like a quick fix or simple solution to an unplanned/unwanted pregnancy. Abortion will not erase reality; it will only take the life of your baby.
- Educate her on the psychological, spiritual, and physical risks of an abortion procedure.
- "Many other women have been in a similar situation to yours and succeeded. They have overcome many obstacles, and if they can do it, you can too."

Reason for Abortion #3: "I'm done with having babies."
Potential Responses:
- "The baby, your new son or daughter, is here, your baby exists." (reinforce reality).
- "This baby is the little sister or little brother to your other children."

- Ask good questions, determine what she means.
- "Let's come up with a plan that will help you with your situation."

Reason for Abortion #4: "*My boyfriend/husband will leave me if I have this baby.*"
Potential Responses:
- "May I speak with your boyfriend/husband and help him understand?"
- "Your boyfriend/husband could also leave you after you have an abortion."
- Studies have shown 70 percent of relationships end after an abortion (in Western countries).
- "If given time and education, your boyfriend/husband could change his mind and decide he wants to be a father."

Reason for Abortion #5: "*My parents are against me having a baby as a single woman.*"
Potential Responses:
- "I understand your parents are against having the baby, but how do you feel about it?" "May I speak with your parents?"
- "Your choices are not between killing your baby and a life on the streets. God has another plan for you."
- Be a Good Samaritan to her. Be ready to do whatever it takes to assist her in this life-and-death crisis. Tell her, "You're not alone. I don't have the answers to this difficult situation, but I will never leave you until we have figured this out."

A woman considering abortion is usually being pressured by the father of the baby, her parents, or others (like the church she attends). None of these people usually have a true understanding of what abortion is and what it does to the baby and the mother. That is why it is so important that you are there to share truth, hope, and life.

Sometimes a woman is facing the possibility of such attacks and ridicule from her church that she considers an abortion is better than being shamed by her church. Too many churches are in the habit of kicking the young woman out of the church if she is pregnant and not married, while doing nothing to the boy or man who got her pregnant. Too many churches are also in the habit of not allowing babies who are conceived out of wedlock to be dedicated or baptized. This is totally wrong! That baby is *not* guilty of any sin. And having a baby out of wedlock is *not* an unpardonable sin. We should *never* be seeking to shame or disgrace a young woman who is pregnant and not married. She was brave enough *not* to have an abortion. She needs our care and support, not our condemnation. We must be full of grace and mercy, and not chase women away just because they are pregnant.

It is our duty to:
- Help people regain a sense of hope in what seems like a hopeless situation.
- Provide factual information about all the options facing them.
- Respectfully educate and encourage them to make a life-affirming decision.
- Always look for an opportunity to share Christ.

Abortion Side Effects: Physical, Emotional, and Spiritual

Abortion kills a baby and can cause great harm to the mother. It can potentially harm her physically, emotionally, and spiritually.

Potential Surgical Complications

A surgical abortion is just that—surgery. And just like any kind of surgery, there are very serious potential risks and complications that a woman must be aware of before having a surgical abortion. We stress that these are potential risks, not risks that are highly likely.

First-and Second-Trimester Abortion Potential Side Effects
- Incomplete abortion
- Infection and bleeding
- Injury to uterus or cervix
- Potential damage to intestines or bladder
- Potential loss of future pregnancies
- Higher risk of infertility
- Future premature delivery
- Maternal death

Though rare, abortion increases the risk of two conditions that can lead to fertility issues: Asherman syndrome and pelvic inflammatory disease (PID). An article in *Healthline* from January 2020 explains Asherman syndrome as a condition where scar tissue builds up inside the uterus. It can be caused by a Dilation and Curettage (D&C) abortion procedure. Women who have had multiple surgical abortions are at greater risk of developing Asherman syndrome and having trouble becoming pregnant in the future. In the first trimester, up to 13 percent of women develop the condition after a D&C. For women who have late-term abortions, the risk jumps to 30 percent.[21]

Potential Chemical Abortion Side Effects
The chemical abortion pill has been documented with many side effects, including hemorrhaging, infection to the point of having blood transfusions, and death.

The Abortion Pill Potential Side Effects
- Heavy bleeding
- Cramping

- Vomiting and diarrhea
- Fever
- Infection
- Death

Morning-After Pill Potential Side Effects
- Nausea or vomiting
- Dizziness
- Fatigue
- Headache
- Breast tenderness
- Bleeding between periods or heavier menstrual bleeding
- Lower abdominal pain or cramps

Potential Traditional Abortion Side Effects
- Hemorrhage
- Infection
- Sepsis—reaction to infection; can cause death
- Peritonitis—a redness and swelling of the tissue that lines your belly or abdomen; may cause death.
- Trauma to the cervix, vagina, uterus, and abdominal organ
- Death

Potential Emotional and Spiritual Side Effects
The emotional and spiritual side effects of abortion may be even more long lasting than the physical side effects. The potential emotional side effects of abortion could include:

- Clinical depression
- Anxiety
- Drug and alcohol abuse
- Eating disorders

- Low self-esteem
- Post-traumatic stress disorder
- Suicidal thoughts and behaviors
- Broken relationships
- Nightmares

While the following information focuses on women, it is very important that we realize that men can feel the heartbreak of abortion just as women can—but perhaps not to the same degree, because it is the woman who has carried that growing baby inside of her. When a woman leaves an abortion clinic after an abortion, she leaves behind the torn pieces of her dead baby and often takes with her a wounded heart. Abortion is a real and traumatic event. The act of ending or allowing someone to end the life of your child in the womb creates the potential for real and lasting emotional damage. With so many cultures normalizing abortion, it forces women to swallow their feelings and does not allow them the chance to grieve the death of their child. Whenever we cannot process a loss in our lives, we cope by trying to diminish the significance of the loss in order to move on. There is a need to understand that abortion causes great damage to the hearts of women, and that healing from that damage can be found in Christ.

After an abortion, some women carry a burden of pain, shame, silence, and heartache. Many struggle for years with repressed memories, guilt, shame, and depression. Women feel they are not allowed to talk about their abortion experience, especially in Church. Many women who have had an abortion suffer from symptoms of post-abortion grief and trauma. Post-traumatic stress is the result of having suffered an event so traumatic that the person is unable to process the event in a *normal* manner. Most often, neither the medical community nor the Church understands abortion as a risk factor in a woman's physical, spiritual, or emotional health.

Certainly, some women, no matter how sure they were about wanting the abortion, come to the point where they understand that the termination of their pregnancy meant the killing of their own child. The shame, anxiety, and guilt associated with the act of having had an abortion can be overwhelming.

Potential Spiritual Side Effects
Because her baby's life was voluntarily surrendered, abortion has a different impact on a woman's heart at a spiritual level. This can cause profound guilt and shame. A person dealing with the long-lasting spiritual damage of abortion needs healing that can only be found in Christ.

Abortion, at its core, is a sin against the Lord—that is the biggest spiritual consequence of engaging in abortion. That sin can lead to shame and guilt. When that sin goes unconfessed, it can lead to a lifetime of pain, shame, and guilt or a hardening of the heart. It can then lead to rebellion against the Lord, and ultimately rejecting God altogether. Some of the spiritual side effects may include:

- Unconfessed sin against God
- Shame and guilt
- Hardening of one's heart
- Rebellion against the Lord
- Rejecting God
- Spiritual death

Abortion Recovery

Millions of women have been wounded by abortion in Africa and worldwide, and they desperately need the healing that can only be found in Christ. The symptoms experienced after an abortion are God's way of letting us know that something is wrong—that there is sin in our life—and the only way to make it right is to turn toward God. Ultimately, abortion is a grave sin, one that grieves the heart of the Lord. Fortunately our heavenly Father sent His Son Jesus Christ to pay the price for *all* our sins. He does not want us to be trapped in the guilt and shame of past sins but instead paved the way for us to have complete freedom from our sins, including abortion. There is *nothing* that can separate us from the love of the Lord. Once we repent, He is ready to immediately restore us to full relationship with Him.

> For I am sure that neither death nor life, nor angels nor rulers, nor things present nor things to come, nor powers, nor height nor depth, nor anything else in all creation, will be able to separate us from the love of God in Christ Jesus our Lord". (Romans 8:38-39, ESV)

Healing from an abortion involves a number of steps that include:

- Repentance
- Confession
- Forgiveness
- Healing
- Restoration

Conclusion

Abortion is the taking of the life of an innocent child developing in the womb. Most people who choose abortion are unaware of the impact it will have on them physically, emotionally, and spiritually. When we are equipped through the Holy Spirit to speak words of wisdom, truth, and love to a woman considering an abortion, we can often encourage them to choose life.

Abortion has caused widespread damage, especially emotionally, to the women who have endured one. With Jesus, we go from heartbroken and hopeless to hopeful. We know we will see our baby in heaven. For women especially, the journey toward being completely healed and restored is just that, a journey. For many women, that journey has included time in an abortion recovery group. This often involves a leader or facilitator who meets with a group of women who have had abortions once a week to guide them through a Bible study about forgiveness, providing them time to repent, confess, and receive forgiveness and healing from their deep wounds.

It is important to note that men also can experience regret, shame, and hurt as a result of abortion and also need to find healing in Christ. It is critical that every church understands the truth about abortion and how it affects men and women, and that churches teach about the sanctity of human life, as well as understand how to offer healing and restoration to those who are dealing with the pain of abortion.

Chapter 8:
Guardians of Life: Global Life-Affirming Ministries

"I hate this baby! I hate this baby!" Those words shook me to my core. The anger and hatred Alisha expressed were palpable. Alisha then assured me that she would have an abortion. I was a young man in my twenties serving as director of a pregnancy center in the United States. I was one of a handful of men running one of the few pregnancy centers in the nation at that time. On this particular day, we only had a few female volunteer counselors, and they all felt this case would be too difficult, so they asked me to see Alisha. The police had brought Alisha to our pregnancy center to have a pregnancy test, one of the many services we offered for free. Alisha's story was horrific. She had been raped and beaten and left half dead. Very similar to the story Jesus told of the Good Samaritan. But I never imagined I would be asked to play the part of the Good Samaritan.

Alisha had just received the news that her test result was positive. She was indeed pregnant as a result of rape, one of the most feared outcomes possible to one of the most horrific acts a human can endure. Her response was completely understandable. The last thing she wanted was to carry the child of the man who had perpetrated such unimaginable violence against her. But in her own words she carried the truth of the situation. She was pregnant with a baby! A person. A human being.

I did the only thing I could do. I prayed. "God, only You know what she is going through. Only You know her fear and pain and suffering. And only You can give me the right words to say. For You have the words of life. Help me, God." And so, realizing that only God could provide what she needed, I started sharing with her. "Alisha," I said, "I can't begin to imagine how you feel. I am a man, and you are a woman. I am Latino, and you are African American. We are very different. So I can't tell you I understand how you feel, or what you are going through. But if the man who violated you were caught, the worst that would happen to him is he would spend time in prison. But you are now planning on ending the life of the baby growing inside of you. That man is guilty of a horrible act of violence against you, but this baby is innocent and has committed no crime. Ending the baby's life by abortion for a crime he or she never committed will not make the pain of your rape lessen. It will only add the pain of knowing that you have ended your baby's life by abortion to the pain of the rape. An abortion will never undo the rape you have endured. And Alisha, I believe God had us here today so I can tell you He loves you and your baby. And I believe that God has allowed this baby to be created inside of you so that one day God will use your baby, if you allow the baby to live, to help take the hatred you now feel out of your heart."

Soon after, Alisha left and I returned to my duties, realizing that I would never forget what had just happened. Several years later I was in my office when I was informed that there was someone in the lobby here to see me. When I went out, to my great surprise, there stood Alisha with her two-year-old son. She proceeded to tell me that everything I had shared with her had come to pass. She no longer had hate in her heart, for this beautiful boy had replaced her

> hatred with love. As I held the boy in my arms, I thanked God for His goodness.
>
> Raúl Reyes
> President
> Life Equip Global

How can the Church respond to the Global Abortion Genocide? The Lord loves us more than we can imagine. As a result of that love, He has provided us with every tool necessary to combat and defeat Satan's Global Abortion Genocide. First, He has given us His Word—the greatest handbook on how we should live our lives. Then, He has given us the Holy Spirit—the Counselor who lives within us and guides our every action. Also, He has given us the Church—the institution made up of Spirit-filled men and women who exist in every village, community, city, and country on Earth. He has also created many kinds of life-affirming ministries around the world.

The pregnancy-related services that churches can provide to help women and men facing an unplanned pregnancy fall into three categories: Prevention, Intervention, and Restoration. *Prevention* involves teaching all ages about biblical sexuality. It equips Christians with Bible-based training to protect them from the sexual attacks of the enemy. Also, it helps to prevent an unplanned pregnancy. *Intervention* involves interceding in a situation where individuals are unsure about the baby they are carrying or are actively considering abortion. Pregnancy centers are an example of intervention. *Restoration* usually involves providing a biblically based program that helps heal the emotional wounds women (and men) receive from abortion. Restoration helps men and women be restored into fellowship with Jesus.

Here are some practical responses that you or your church might decide to implement to equip the Church and to defend innocent preborn lives. These are just examples. The Lord may call you to respond in a totally different and unique manner. We strongly recommend that you pray about starting one or more of these life-affirming ministries through your church. Association for Life of Africa (AFLA) or Life Equip Global can provide you with guidance as you get started and can connect you with experts who can provide further guidance in how to launch one of these ministries.

Prevention Ministries

a. Biblical Sexual Integrity Classes—Teach your congregation what the Bible says about sexuality. This can be done by separating men and women and teaching the youth separate from adults. Life Equip Global has a resource available called "Sex, Life and Death, and the Bible," which is a curriculum for adults on biblical sexuality.

i. Equipping Godly Men—Teach men to be not only sexually pure but encourage them to lead and teach younger men, and to an example of godly purity.

ii. Equipping Godly Women—Teach women to be not only sexually pure but encourage them to lead and teach younger women, and to be an example of godly purity.

iii. Youngsters and Adolescents—Prepare them for all the temptations they could face.

b. Marriage and Family Class—Teach what the Bible says about marriage and what it means to have a godly biblical family.

c. Mentoring Young Men and Women—A program where young men and women are discipled by older men and women and taught how to grow in godly wisdom, especially in sexual areas.

d. School-Based Abstinence Program—Creating a program on the importance and benefits of waiting for sex until you are married and teaching the program in schools.

e. **Parenting Class**—Teaching men and women the basics about having and raising babies.

f. **Fetal Development Teaching**—Teaching men and women all about the miracle of creation and how a baby develops in the womb.

g. **Sports Team/Teaching Club/Hobby Club with Abstinence Training**—Offer young men and women (sometimes street children) any kind of sports-oriented or teaching program in exchange for their participating in a church-taught abstinence training.

Intervention Ministries

a. **Life Advocate Training**—Offer Life Advocate Training to church members so they can choose life and help others choose life.

b. **Pregnancy Ministry**—Training women in your church with Life Advocate Training so they can assist someone who is in an unplanned or unwanted pregnancy.

c. **Pregnancy Center**—A place where a woman can go to receive a pregnancy test, counseling, and practical assistance (baby clothes, diapers, etc.) so that she can find hope and carry her baby to term.

d. **Prenatal Clinic**—A medical clinic, usually in partnership with a pregnancy center, where a woman can receive medical care for her pregnancy and where delivery of the baby is also provided.

Restoration Ministries

a. **Abortion Recovery Ministry**—A Bible study on forgiveness, helping women be fully healed from the emotional wounds of a past abortion.

b. **Home for Unwed Mothers with a Teaching Program**—A place where a woman with a newborn child with no support system can stay. This program can be combined with a job-training program that provides the young mother with the training necessary to get a job or start her own business.

Other Ministries

a. Host a Baby Shower—A baby shower is a party of gift-giving for the pregnant mother where she can receive baby furniture, baby clothes, baby diapers, baby bottles, and baby formula. It celebrates the delivery or expected birth of a child or the transformation of a woman into a mother.

b. Clothing Closet—A place in the church where supplies for a pregnant woman are kept for distribution. The clothing closet might include baby clothes, baby furniture, baby food, or other baby-related items.

c. Job Training—A program where women (or men) are taught skills that assist them in acquiring a job. Examples of job-training programs include teaching them how to cook, computer skills, raise chickens, or sew.

d. Food Pantry—A place in the church where cans of food or other food items can be kept and given to poor people or families in difficulty.

e. Female Hygiene and Fertility Education—Teaching women the benefits of female hygiene and the reproductive cycle. Including the topic of fertility in biblical sex education for adults and teens comes with huge potential benefits. Using cycle beads to teach the fertility cycle is a powerful and helpful tool.

f. Daycare—Providing young women with care for their baby while they work so they can provide for their family.

Pregnancy Ministries

After reading this book, you might be thinking to yourself, *What's my next step?* We strongly recommend that you and your prayer partners take some time—it could be a day, a week, a month, or a year—to seek the Lord in prayer. Read the Word, and listen closely to what the Lord is asking you to do. Then, if you feel led to respond with a pregnancy ministry (like a pregnancy center), this section will prove helpful.

Pregnancy centers are a Christian ministry. The most important duty they have is to share the Gospel of Jesus Christ at every opportunity, while encouraging those facing an unwanted pregnancy to choose life. Pregnancy centers often have one paid Center Director. Depending on the size of the ministry, additional staff and many volunteers help with the many duties needed at a pregnancy center. Pregnancy centers are usually designated as NGOs or nonprofit organizations and usually have a Board of Directors that provides leadership and guidance. They are often supported by a combination of individual donors, churches, grants, and sometimes government funds. Pregnancy centers are staffed by a leadership team, usually consisting of a Center Director and—depending on the size of the ministry and the number of clients they minister to—additional staff.

In most pregnancy center models, the staff is compensated financially, but some pregnancy centers use only volunteers. In addition to a leadership team or staff, pregnancy centers usually engage the use of volunteers to assist in a variety of ways, assisting with administrative functions or ministering to clients.

Most pregnancy centers offer all their services free of charge to the women they serve. Some of these services may include:

- Pregnancy tests
- Education on pregnancy, abortion, and adoption
- Childbirth and parenting classes
- Mentoring mothers and fathers
- Post-abortive recovery groups
- Referrals
- Emergency assistance such as diapers, formula, and maternity and baby clothing

Types of pregnancy ministries you might prayerfully consider starting include:

Life Advocates
Life Advocate Training is a free online training through Life Equip Global. Individuals who have gone through the Life Advocate Training are called Life Advocates, Christians who are prepared to share truth, hope, and the love of Christ to anyone considering abortion.

Church-Based Pregnancy Center
A church-based pregnancy ministry or pregnancy center is a ministry created as an outreach of an individual church. Pregnancy centers may be located on church properties or may have their own independent offices or locations.

Traditional Pregnancy Center
Traditional pregnancy centers offer the same services as church-based pregnancy centers, although they often have expanded services. These types of pregnancy centers are usually not located on church property. They are usually found in a leased or owned building, facility, or office space. Traditional pregnancy centers often are supported by a number of different churches as well as donations from many Christians. They may also have annual fundraising events.

Medical Pregnancy Centers
Medical pregnancy centers provide most of the services provided by traditional pregnancy centers, but also provide additional medical services. In most medical models, a center employs medically trained staff—nurses and doctor—who are compensated financially. Some medical centers also use volunteer medical staff. In addition to a leadership team or staff, pregnancy centers usually engage the use of

volunteers to assist in a variety of ways. This includes assisting with administrative functions and ministering to clients.

In addition to the services provided by traditional pregnancy centers, medical pregnancy centers may also provide:

- Sonograms
- Prenatal care
- STD testing
- Well-woman care
- Pap smears
- Breast exams
- Other medical services

Mobile Pregnancy Centers

Mobile pregnancy centers are pregnancy centers operating in some type of vehicle; they provide many of the services of a traditional pregnancy center, which usually includes the ability to provide ultrasounds. Mobile pregnancy centers provide an effective way to reach those in remote locations. Since a mobile pregnancy center is providing Christian ministry, the most important duty it has is to lovingly and with respect share the Gospel of Jesus Christ at every opportunity to those they serve and encourage those facing an unplanned pregnancy to choose life.

Mobile pregnancy centers can be an extension of an existing church, traditional or medical pregnancy center, or its own ministry. Mobile pregnancy center ministries are usually run under the direction of a Board of Directors of an NGO. They are often supported by a combination of individual donors, churches, grants, and sometimes government funds.

Mobile pregnancy centers are staffed by a driver and staff member who will provide services, sometimes including a nurse-sonographer.

In most mobile pregnancy center models, the staff is compensated financially. However, it is possible to have all volunteer staff. Mobile pregnancy centers serve women who want to find out if they are pregnant. One of the services offered is a pregnancy test and, if the woman is far enough along, an ultrasound.

Services are provided free of charge and may include:

- Pregnancy tests
- Ultrasounds
- Education on pregnancy, abortion, and adoption

Having a mobile pregnancy center brings ultrasounds and the message of Christ and life to pregnant girls and women who may not be able to be reached otherwise.

When starting a life-affirming ministry of any kind, we strongly recommend you start with a simple model that requires little or no financial support and which you and some of your Christian friends can do together. At the end of this book is a list of ministries in Africa that can assist you in starting a pregnancy center or life-affirming ministry. Some of the more advanced models, like a traditional pregnancy center or a medical pregnancy center, may be perfect for a ministry, a church, or a group of churches to undertake—especially if you live in an area where abortions are prevalent and there is a good public transportation system.

Life Equip Global—Bringing the Life Message to the Church

The story at the beginning of this chapter occurred almost forty years ago. I now have the privilege of leading an international ministry called Life Equip Global. This is a ministry that the Lord laid on my heart many years ago. The heart of Life Equip Global is a burning desire to see others come to Christ in the mission field created by abortion, while helping mothers make life-saving decisions for their babies. The world is experiencing the greatest destruction of innocent human lives in history through a Global Abortion Genocide. Life Equip Global recognizes and strongly believes that it is through the Church of Jesus Christ that His love, truth, and mercy will be shared with this lost and hurting world. That is why we exist: to equip the Church with a life-saving message.

As we work to save lives from abortion while sharing the Gospel of Christ, we experience never-before-seen opportunities for countless individuals to be won for Christ. The multiplication of technology to every corner of the globe provides the means by which we can multiply our ability to save lives and share Christ globally. This allows maximum impact with minimal expense. The approximately seventy-three million babies killed annually by abortion is a Global Abortion Genocide.[1] This presents an opportunity to save millions of lives from abortion and bring countless numbers of hurting women and men to Christ. In order to do so, the Church must be equipped with the training and the resources to respond to the horror of abortion and defend and proclaim life. This is the mission of Life Equip Global. We equip pastors and Christian leaders globally with a Christ-centered sanctity of human life training.

Our primary focus is reaching the church in Africa, because this is where God is most powerfully at work. By equipping Christians around the globe, and especially in Africa, to respond to the Global Abortion Genocide and by preparing them to train others, we can radically change the number of babies being killed by abortion. *The Church is God's response to the Global Abortion Genocide.*

Life Equip Global
- Equips the body of Christ to promote biblical sexuality, defend the sanctity of human life, and help heal the wounds caused by abortion.

- Is evangelical, missional, and Christ-centered.
- Makes the knowledge, training, and resources developed over the last forty years of serving in the mission field created by abortion available to Christians worldwide.
- Distributes Christ-centered, life-saving training and resources to Christian leaders who then distribute the information, training, and resources to their own networks.

By equipping the church globally, it can launch prevention, intervention, and restoration ministries that prepare believers to respond with hope, life, and the Gospel of Jesus Christ to anyone in the world who is considering ending the life of their child through abortion. Life Equip Global collaborates with other Christian nonprofit organizations and churches in Africa and around the world to establish a network of training resources for the Church to be the primary defender of life. By training the Church, we expand the message that all life is valuable and that Christ is the answer to whatever issue we face. By equipping the Church, Life Equip Global multiplies the message of life to respond to the Global Abortion Genocide.

Life Equip Global Goals
- Provide resources to equip the Church, ministries, and individuals to save lives and share the Gospel.
- See Christ-centered Sanctity of Human Life (SOHL) ministries multiply globally.
- See people come to new life in Christ, preborn lives saved from abortion, and the wounded healed from the damage of abortion.

Life Equip Global Distinctives:
- We exist to draw people to Christ.
- We create pro-life resources to be shared with the Church.
- We use technology to maximize impact and minimize expense.

- We utilize high-level volunteer trainers to minimize expense.
- We train international and national leaders to become self-sustaining.
- We identify and partner with existing Christian ministry networks.

Global Life Academy
Life Equip Global has an online Global Life Academy, which is the leading online platform for international Christian leaders to receive comprehensive Christian pro-life resources. These resources include comprehensive training seminars focused on prevention, intervention, and restoration. These resources are available through recorded online sessions, through live teachers using Zoom, are downloadable in print or audio format, or from in-person trainings led by national Life Advocate Trainers. You are strongly encouraged to attend the Global Life Academy and become a part of the solution. Become equipped to proclaim the biblical truth that *all* life, starting at conception, is to be valued and protected.

Life Equip Global invites you to attend classes and training on our online Global Life Academy. Global Life Academy offers online classes which you can take from a live expert or by watching one of our prerecorded videos. You can also download the training in written form or listen to a training in an audio format. If getting on the internet is a challenge you can't overcome, reach out to us through email or WhatsApp, and we will let you know if there is an in-person training being offered near you. All graduates of our training classes receive a certificate from Global Life Academy.

Our training classes include:

- Prevention
- Sex, Life and Death, and the Bible
- The Role of Men

- The Bible and Marriage
- More Than Sex (curriculum for youth)
- Intervention
- Life Advocate Training—Part 1
- Life Advocate Training—Part 2
- Restoration—Break Every Chain—Abortion Recovery
- Ministry Application
- Starting a Pregnancy Center
- Starting a Mobile Pregnancy Center
- Starting an Abortion Recovery Program
- Starting a Maternity Home
- Other Life-Affirming Ministries

Desired Outcomes

Life Equip Global's desired outcomes are to see people come to new life in Christ, preborn lives saved from abortion, people equipped to abstain from sex until they are married, and the wounded healed from the damage of abortion. We also wish our work to result in Christ-centered sanctity of human life ministries launched through the Church globally. The ultimate goal is to see the Church embracing and teaching the sanctity of human life as a core biblical truth.

Sharing the Gospel

The heart of Life Equip Global is sharing the Gospel of Jesus Christ. Evangelism is proclaiming the Good News that God created us, knows us and our circumstances, loves us, and through Jesus Christ has established the way to be restored into relationship with Him.

When the Lord opens the door for us to have a discussion with others, the most important thing we can offer anyone is a path to a relationship with God through Jesus Christ. A person considering an abortion is in the middle of a crisis. And a person in a crisis needs a lifeline—they need good news—the Good News of Jesus.

They are more likely to receive this ultimate truth as they face a time of ultimate need.

Sharing the Good News—also known as the Gospel of Jesus Christ—is one of the most important works any believer in Christ can do. We read in Mark, "He said to them, 'Go into all the world and preach the gospel to all creation'" (Mark 16:15).

How to Proclaim the Gospel
- Pray—As children of God, prayer is always our first step.
- Engage—Start a conversation.
- Listen—This is a very important part of a conversation.
- Teachable Moment—When we are led by the Holy Spirit to move the conversation to a spiritual discussion and then proclaim the Good News.

Before sharing the Gospel, remember that you earn the right to be heard by first listening. Sharing the Gospel is often most effective after one has spent time talking with and listening to the other person. You will learn more about becoming a better communicator in Lesson Four. Win a person, not an argument.

There are many ways to share the Good News of Jesus. One powerful way to share the Gospel is simply to share your testimony. In the hymn "Amazing Grace" it states, "I once was lost, but now I'm found." It's as simple as that. Explain how you were once lost and now you are found. Explain what your life was like before Jesus. Explain why and how you came to Jesus. And explain what difference Jesus has made in your life.

Most people will recognize that there is sin in their life. People need salvation because God is perfect and holy but we are sinful, and He cannot accept sinners in their sinful state in heaven. All of us are imperfect. All of us are sinners. You can start by telling them why they need to be saved in the first place.

> For all have sinned and fall short of the glory of God. (Romans 3:23)

> For the wages of sin is death, but the gift of God is eternal life in Christ Jesus our Lord. (Romans 6:23)

Every person has been found guilty of sin—which separates us from God—and the payment for our sin is death. Not just physical death, but eternal death in the form of being separated from God for all eternity.

> He will punish those who do not know God and do not obey the gospel of our Lord Jesus. They will be punished with everlasting destruction and shut out from the presence of the Lord and from the glory of his might. (2 Thessalonians 1:8-9)

This prepares us to now share the Good News.

> But God demonstrates his own love for us in this: While we were still sinners, Christ died for us. (Romans 5:8)

> For God so loved the world that He gave His only begotten Son, that whoever believes in Him should not perish but have everlasting life. For God did not send His Son into the world to condemn the world, but that the world through Him might be saved. (John 3:16-17, NKJV)

God loves us so much that He sent His Son Jesus—who is perfect and without sin—to die in our place, to pay for our sins. The price for our sin has been paid for by Jesus Himself. All we must now do is believe in Jesus and accept the gift of eternal life that is in Christ Jesus. Jesus paid with His life for our sins; we should now live for Him.

Everyone must understand that you cannot earn salvation through doing good deeds. "For it is by grace you have been saved, through faith—and this is not from yourselves, it is the gift of God" (Ephesians 2:8). Salvation cannot be earned. If salvation could be earned, then Jesus didn't need to die. God could have just waited for people to earn their salvation.

When a person accepts and believes in Jesus as their Savior, God gives them the free gift of salvation. That is the Good News of the Gospel. The gift of eternal life is free—*but a gift must be accepted.*

You can now ask the person, "Do you believe in Jesus as your Savior? Do you trust Jesus has paid for your sins, and do you wish to receive God's free gift of eternal life?" If they say yes, you can ask them to repeat a prayer after you.

Here is a prayer you may wish to use.

Jesus, I believe You are the Son of God. I know that I am a sinner, and my sins have separated me from You. I know that the price for sin is death. And I believe You paid for my sins at the cross through Your death. I ask for Your forgiveness. Thank you for bearing my sins and giving me the gift of eternal life. I invite You to come into my heart and life. Come into my heart, Lord Jesus, and be my Savior. Amen.

Remember, it's not the prayer that saves; it's the belief and faith behind the prayer that lay hold of salvation. Once we come to faith in Jesus, then we are filled by the Holy Spirit. Then comes the process of being transformed from the inside out. *Sharing the Gospel is where hope is birthed.*

Life Equip Global in Africa

Our focus starts in Africa where the arms of the Church are opened wide and where God is powerfully at work. Africa is also where five to eight million babies are being killed each year through abortion.

For the last three years, we have been training pastors to train others. As the number of trainers multiply, the message of life will multiply through the Church in Africa. As a result of awakening the Church to its role and responsibilities in regard to defending innocent human life, we expect to see prevention, intervention, and restoration ministries multiply exponentially in Africa. When the world starts knocking on Africa's door requesting Africans to immigrate, our prayer is that they will bring both the Gospel of Christ and the gospel of life with them to the whole world.

Our strategy for coming alongside the growing Church in Africa is to respectfully offer whatever training and equipping we can to local pastors and leaders. We realize that they are by far the best equipped to hear from the Lord and put ministries like pregnancy centers into place that deal with the issues in regard to the Global Abortion Genocide. We desire to see healthy, indigenous, reproducing, self-sustaining, life-affirming ministries start and grow in Africa. We do not want to repeat the mistakes made in the past by Western Christians that made Africans dependent upon the West for financial support. We strongly believe that the Lord will provide the resources necessary in the countries where He has called Christians to act.

Africa Life Strategy

Our strategy in Africa starts with the Africa Life Coordinator (ALC) who is Life Equip Global's primary representative in Africa and who, in partnership with the President, helps create and implement a strategy for multiplying the message of life throughout the Church in Africa. The ALC helps recruit, train, and lead a team of National Life Coordinators (NLCs). National Life Coordinators are trained to be self-sustaining and help multiply Life Advocate Trainings in their regions and countries. As a result of awakening the Church to its responsibilities in regard to defending innocent human life, we expect to see prevention, intervention, and restoration ministries multiply throughout Africa.

The African Awakening Small Group Bible Study

Another resource Life Equip Global offers is *The African Awakening* Small Group Bible Study, which is a thought-provoking and timely study that delves into the profound insights presented in this book. The purpose of *The African Awakening* Small Group Bible Study is to explore the spiritual and biblical perspectives on the demographic challenges the world will soon be facing, and how these challenges intersect with God's plan for His people. Through engaging discussions and scriptural exploration, participants will gain a deeper understanding of the implications of the Global Abortion Genocide and discern God's call to action.

Conclusion

To address the issue of abortion in Africa effectively, we need to emphasize the need for compassionate outreach. This involves supporting pregnancy centers, offering counseling services, and creating awareness about the alternatives to abortion. By extending practical support and care to women (and men) facing unplanned pregnancies, we seek to empower and equip them to make life-affirming choices. Abortion in Africa is a grave concern that challenges the fundamental belief in the sanctity of life. The statistics from recent years reflect the magnitude of the issue and highlight the urgency for compassionate action. We must advocate for the provision of spiritual, emotional, financial, and medical support to women facing challenging circumstances, helping them to choose life for their unborn children. By promoting a culture of life, engaging in Bible-led discussions, and providing practical support, we can protect the rights and dignity of both the unborn *and* women facing unexpected pregnancies in Africa.

With the world facing an imminent crisis due to explosive abortion numbers and other issues causing a plummeting population, it is imperative that we focus on Africa, where the largest Church in the world is growing and hungry to receive sanctity of human life training. We invite you to join Life Equip Global in this historic move of God and, together, to do battle against the satanic Global Abortion Genocide. Take advantage of our many free and transformational classes and, after getting certified, teach these life-saving trainings to others. If the Lord has blessed you financially, become a Global Life Partner with Life Equip Global, so that together we can bless the Church and bring life to a broken world. You will find information at the back of this book on how to join an upcoming Life Advocate Training Class, start an *African Awakening* small group using our *African Awakening* guidebook, or become a Global Life Partner. You will also find organizations like the Association for Life of Africa who can come alongside you with vital training on how to start a pregnancy center in your church, community, or city. There are countless women like Alisha in your country that need the love of Christ.

About the Author

Raúl Reyes has a local, national, and international reputation for keeping Christ at the center of a pro-life message designed to equip the Church for life. Because of his forty years in sanctity of human life ministry, Raúl is widely viewed as an authority on abortion, the Church's role in defending the sanctity of human life, starting and multiplying life-affirming ministries such as pregnancy centers, and equipping the body of Christ internationally with life-saving resources and training.

Raúl has led some of the largest pro-life ministries in the United States including New Life Solutions in Florida, Life Network in Colorado, and Choices Pregnancy Centers in Arizona. While at Choices, Raúl launched one of the first fully prenatal pregnancy center ministries (with four locations) in the U.S. Over the course of the last three decades, Raúl has also taught many seminars at the Heartbeat International and Care Net conferences. Raúl has also served in a national capacity as Special Assistant to Dr. James Dobson at Focus on the Family, where he represented Focus on the Family to Hispanic donors in the United States.

Internationally, Raúl has traveled the world helping establish a network of pregnancy centers, training boards, and staff as well as teaching thousands of pastors and Christian leaders in over twenty countries regarding the sanctity of human life. Currently, Raúl is on the board of Care Net as well as Hope Pregnancy Clinic in Puerto Rico. Raúl is the Founder and President of Life Equip Global, which provides high-quality and effective online training and resources on the sanctity of human life to the Church globally. Raúl also recently became the Vice President of International Affairs for Choose Life Marketing, the largest Christian pro-life marketing agency in the world.

Raúl is ordained through Calvary Chapel. Raúl travels frequently as a guest speaker both nationally and internationally. Raúl has been married to Christine, his partner in ministry, for forty-three years. Raúl and Christine received Heartbeat International's 2023 Servant Leadership Award. They have five children and eight grandchildren and live in Colorado Springs, Colorado.

Get In Touch

If you have been touched by this book, have examples of life-giving ministries, or just want to reach out, we would love to hear from you. We are all on a journey together and have much to learn from one another. If you are a Christian ministry leader, we also have many resources available on our Life Equip Global website.

Please reach out to us to sign up for an upcoming training, to share your story about how Life Advocate Training has impacted you, to share a story about how God used you to save a life using Life Advocate Training, or to share your personal story of abortion in your life.

You can find out about the many wonderful pro-life ministries serving Africa on our website.

Choose Life Marketing, the world's largest pro-life marketing agency, also stands ready to help you take your pro-life ministry, church, or Christian organization to the next level. Contact Choose Life Marketing at info@chooselifemarketing.com. Or call them at 573-445-9295.

If you or someone you know has been hurt as a result of an abortion, reach out to Surrendering the Secret at surrenderingthesecret.com to find out about an upcoming Abortion Healing Bible Study.

Go to www.lifeequipglobal.org to sign-up for:
- More Than Sex—Sexual Integrity Curriculum
- Life Advocate Training (Part 1 and Part 2)
- Break Every Chain—Healing from Abortion Bible Study

To order copies of *The African Awakening*:
In Africa, contact Bramuel Musya
bmusya@lifeequipglobal.org

In the U.S., go to Amazon.com

To donate to Life Equip Global:
Please visit https://lifeequipglobal.org/donate/

Or contact us at:
Life Equip Global
PO Box 88050
Colorado Springs, CO 80908

By email you can reach us at:
info@lifeequipglobal.org

Be sure to follow Raúl on his Facebook page, Raúl Reyes.

Endnotes

Preface

1. James Gallagher, "Fertility rate: 'Jaw-dropping' global crash in children being born," BBC, July 14, 2020, https://www.bbc.com/news/health-53409521.

Chapter 1: The Global Abortion Genocide

1. Patrick Thonneau, Nathalie Goyaux, Segbegnon Goufodji, and Johanne Sundby, "Abortion and Maternal Mortality in Africa," *New England Journal of Medicine* 347, no. 24 (December 12, 2002): 1984–85, https://doi.org/10.1056/nejm200212123472420.
2. Wikipedia, s.v. "World War II Casualties," last modified May 28, 2024, https://en.wikipedia.org/wiki/World_War_II_casualties.
3. "Unintended Pregnancy and Abortion Worldwide," Guttmacher Institute, accessed April 4, 2024, https://www.guttmacher.org/fact-sheet/induced-abortion-worldwide#:~:text=This%20translates%20to%2073%20million%20abortions%20per%20year.
4. John MacArthur, "The Biblical View on Abortion, Part 1," Grace to You, August 30, 1992, https://www.gty.org/library/sermons-library/90-67/the-biblical-view-on-abortion-part-1.
5. Definition of The Sanctity of Human Life written by Raúl Reyes.
6. "Unintended Pregnancy and Abortion Worldwide," Guttmacher Institute
7. "Abortion Statistics: United States Data and Trends," National Right to Life Educational Foundation, accessed April 4, 2024, https://nrlc.org/uploads/factsheets/FS01AbortionintheUS.pdf.
8. "National Estimate of Abortion in India Released," Guttmacher Institute, December 11, 2017, https://www.guttmacher.org/news-release/2017/national-estimate-abortion-india-released. https://www.guttmacher.org/news-release/2017/national-estimate-abortion-india-released.
9. "National Estimate of Abortion in India Released," Guttmacher Institute, December 11, 2017, https://www.guttmacher.org/news-release/2017/national-estimate-abortion-india-released.

10. David Batty, "13 Million Abortions Carried Out Every Year in China, Newspaper Reveals," Guardian, July 30, 2009, https://www.theguardian.com/world/2009/jul/30/china-abortion-statistics.
12. "Mifepristone for Abortion in a Global Context: Safe, Effective and Approved in Nearly 100 Countries," Guttmacher Institute, accessed April 4, 2024, https://www.guttmacher.org/2023/07/mifepristone-abortion-global-context-safe-effective-and-approved-nearly-100-countries.
13. "Abortion in Africa," Guttmacher Institute, accessed April 4, 2024, https://www.guttmacher.org/fact-sheet/abortion-africa.
14. "Evidence on Abortion Status and Trends Across Sub-Saharan Africa: Guttmacher and AFIDEP Session at FIGO 2020 Congress," AFIDEP, accessed April 4, 2024, https://www.afidep.org/unintended-pregnancy-and-unsafe-abortion-in-sub-saharan-africa-new-report-by-guttmacher-institute/.
15. "Abortion in Africa," Guttmacher Institute

Chapter 2: Crossroad of Death: The Intersection Between Africa and Abortion

1. "Abortions Are Legal in Much of Africa, but Few Women May Be Aware, and Providers Don't Advertise It," USNews.com, April 2, 2024, https://www.usnews.com/news/world/articles/2024-04-02/abortions-are-legal-in-much-of-africa-but-few-women-may-be-aware-and-providers-dont-advertise-it.
2. "Abortions Are Legal in Much of Africa," USNews.com.
3. "The Cradle of Humankind World Heritage Site," Cradle of Humankind, accessed April 5, 2024, https://www.maropeng.co.za/content/page/introduction-to-your-visit-to-the-cradle-of-humankind-world-heritage-site.
4. "About Us," Center for Reproductive Rights, accessed April 5, 2024, https://reproductiverights.org/about-us/.
5. Graeme Reid, "Progress and Setbacks on LGBT Rights in Africa—An Overview of the Last Year," *Daily Maverick*, June 22, 2022, https://www.hrw.org/news/2022/06/22/progress-and-setbacks-lgbt-rights-africa-overview-last-year.

6. Reproductive Rights and Abortion, Human Rights Watch, accessed April 5, 2024, https://www.hrw.org/topic/womens-rights/reproductive-rights-and-abortion.
7. S D Mumford and E Kessel, "Role of abortion in control of global population growth," *Clinics in obstetrics and gynaecology* vol. 13,1 (1986): 19-31, accessed April 5, 2024, https://pubmed.ncbi.nlm.nih.gov/3709011/.
8. Stephen Emmott, "Humans: the real threat to life on Earth," *The Guardian*, June 29, 2013, https://www.theguardian.com/environment/2013/jun/30/stephen-emmott-ten-billion.
9. Olivia Nater, "Population growth and climate change threaten African nature," *Population Connection*, July 21, 2022, https://populationconnection.org/blog/population-growth-and-climate-change-threaten-african-nature/.
10. Graeme Reid, "'Traditional Values': A Potent Weapon Against LGBT Rights," *Emerging Europe*, November 4, 2017, https://www.hrw.org/news/2017/11/06/traditional-values-potent-weapon-against-lgbt-rights.
11. "Gender and sexual orientation diversity in children and adolescents in schools," American Psychological Association, September 13, 2021, https://www.apa.org/pi/lgbt/resources/diversity-schools.
12. Elizabeth Perry, "LGBTQ acceptance across the globe: 5 ways to encourage change," *BetterUp*, May 26, 2022, https://www.betterup.com/blog/lgbtq-acceptance.
13. Action Change, "Fighting for LGBTQ+ Rights in Africa," Global Giving, accessed April 8, 2024, https://www.globalgiving.org/projects/fight-for-lgbtq-rights-in-africa/.
14. "The Democratic Republic of the Congo Leads the Way on Abortion Access: A Pathway for Reproductive Rights Advocates in Francophone Africa," Population Reference Bureau (PRB), October 28, 2021, https://www.prb.org/resources/the-democratic-republic-of-the-congo-leads-the-way-on-abortion-access-a-pathway-for-reproductive-rights-advocates-in-francophone-africa/.
15. Lucia Pizzarossa, Michelle Maziwisa, and Ebenezer Durojaye, "Self-Managed Abortion in Africa: The Decriminalization Imperative in Regional Human Rights Standards," *Health and Human Rights*

Journal, vol 25(1) (May 14, 2023): 171-183, https://www.hhrjournal.org/2023/05/self-managed-abortion-in-africa-the-decriminalization-imperative-in-regional-human-rights-standards/.

16. Eve Brecker, Meghan Reidy, Rebecca Rosenberg, Imelda Zosa-Feranil, Shiza Farid, Parfait Eloundou-Enyegue, Gorrety Parmu, and Haley Brahmbhatt, "2022: The Future of Family Planning in Africa," Population Reference Bureau (PRB), May 9, 2022, https://www.prb.org/resources/the-future-of-family-planning-in-africa/.

17. "Providing Quality Family Planning Services," *Center for Disease Control and Prevention MMWR,* vol 63, no. 4 (April 25, 2014), https://opa.hhs.gov/sites/default/files/2020-10/providing-quality-family-planning-services-2014_1.pdf.

18. "Addressing Barriers to Safe Abortion," International Federation of Gynecology and Obstetrics, accessed April 9, 2024, https://www.figo.org/resources/figo-statements/addressing-barriers-safe-abortion.

19. Marge Berer, "Making Abortions Safe: A Matter of Good Public Health Policy and Practice," *Reproductive Health Matters* 10, no. 19 (2002): 31–44. doi:10.1016/S0968-8080(02)00021-6, https://www.tandfonline.com/doi/full/10.1016/S0968-8080%2802%2900021-6.

20. "The U.S. Government and International Family Planning & Reproductive Health Efforts," Global Health Policy, January 2, 2024, https://www.kff.org/global-health-policy/fact-sheet/the-u-s-government-and-international-family-planning-reproductive-health-efforts/.

21. https://www.icrw.org/the-global-abortion-movement-perspectives-from-africa-and-beyond/

22. "Could Uganda Be the Garden of Eden?" Africa and Beyond, July 18, 2021, https://www.africa-and-beyond.co.uk/blog/could-uganda-be-the-garden-of-eden/.

23. Quamrul Ashraf and Oded Galor, "The 'Out of Africa' Hypothesis, Human Genetic Diversity, and Comparative Economic Development," *The American economic review* vol. 103,1 (2013): 1-46, doi:10.1257/aer.103.1.1, https://www.ncbi.nlm.nih.gov/pmc/articles/PMC4262934/#:~:text=According%20

to%20this%20well%2Destablished,beginning%20about%2070%2C000%E2%80%9390%2C000%20BP.
24. Ibrahim B. Anoba, "How a Population of 4.2 Billion Could Impact Africa by 2100: The Possible Economic, Demographic, and Geopolitical Outcomes," The SAIS Review of International Affairs, Septmeber 24, 2019, https://saisreview.sais.jhu.edu/how-a-population-of-4-2-billion-could-impact-africa-by-2100-the-possible-economic-demographic-and-geopolitical-outcomes/.
25. "Population Facts," United Nations, December 2019, https://www.un.org/en/development/desa/population/publications/pdf/popfacts/PopFacts_2019-6.pdf.
26. "Our Work in Africa," UN Environment Programme, accessed April 9, 2024, https://www.unep.org/regions/africa/our-work-africa#:~:text=Africa%20is%20home%20to%20some,of%20its%20chromium%20and%20platinum.
27. "Valuable People: Debunking the Myth of Overpopulation," Cato Institute, November/December 2022, https://www.cato.org/policy-report/november/december-2022/valuable-people-debunking-myth-overpopulation#:~:text=One%20of%20the%20most%20popular,human%20action%20and%20economic%20progress.
28. Philomena Mwaura, "The Family in Africa," EWTN, accessed April 9, 2024, https://www.ewtn.com/catholicism/library/family-in-africa-3973.
29. "The U.S. Government and Global Health," Global Health Policy, September 26, 2022, https://www.kff.org/global-health-policy/fact-sheet/the-u-s-government-and-global-health/.
30. "International Planned Parenthood Federation Africa Region," Hewlett Foundation, accessed April 9, 2024, https://hewlett.org/grants/international-planned-parenthood-federation-africa-region-for-support-of-ippf-aros-abortion-work-in-francophone-west-africa/.
31. Siri Suh, "A Stalled Revolution? Misoprostol and the Pharmaceuticalization of Reproductive Health in Francophone Africa," *Frontiers in sociology* vol. 6 590556, April 12, 2021, doi:10.3389/fsoc.2021.590556, https://www.ncbi.nlm.nih.gov/pmc/articles/PMC8091168/.

32. Boniface Ushie and Kenneth Juma, "How US policy on abortion affects women in Africa," *The Conversation*, May 6, 2022, https://theconversation.com/how-us-policy-on-abortion-affects-women-in-africa-182525
33. "Fact Sheet: U.S.-Africa Partnership in Health Cooperation," The White House, December 13, 2022, https://www.whitehouse.gov/briefing-room/statements-releases/2022/12/13/fact-sheet-u-s-africa-partnership-in-health-cooperation/.
34. Martin Armstrong, "Abortion in Africa: 28 Years of Progress," *Statista*, May 18, 2022, https://www.statista.com/chart/27472/abortion-legal-status-african-countries-timeline/.
35. "Africa's Unsafe Abortions," National Library of Medicine 21,1 (November 1998): 43, https://pubmed.ncbi.nlm.nih.gov/12294918/.
36. Aaron Earls, "7 Encouraging Trends in Global Christianity for 2023," Lifeway Research, September 19, 2023, https://research.lifeway.com/2023/09/19/7-encouraging-trends-in-global-christianity-for-2023/.

Chapter 3: Vanishing World: The Global Population Crisis

1. Ben Turner, "World's population could plummet to 6 billion by the end of the century, study suggests," Live Science, March 30, 2023, https://www.livescience.com/worlds-population-could-plummet-to-six-billion-by-the-end-of-the-century-new-study-suggests.
2. Countries with Declining Population 2024, World Population Review, accessed April 13, 2024, https://worldpopulationreview.com/country-rankings/countries-with-declining-population.
3. Anthony Cilluffo and Neil G. Ruiz, "World's population is projected to nearly stop growing by the end of the century," Pew Research Center, June 17, 2019, https://www.pewresearch.org/short-reads/2019/06/17/worlds-population-is-projected-to-nearly-stop-growing-by-the-end-of-the-century/.
4. Cilluffo and Ruiz, "World's population is projected to nearly stop growing by the end of the century," Pew Research Center

5. J Craig, "Replacement level fertility and future population growth," National Library of Medicine, 78 (Winter 1994): 20–2, https://pubmed.ncbi.nlm.nih.gov/7834459/#:~:text=PIP%3A%20%20Replacement%20level%20fertility%20is,of%202.1%20children%20%20per%20woman.
6. Helen Davidson, "China populatin decline accelerates as birthrate hits record low," Guardian, January 17, 2024, https://www.theguardian.com/world/2024/jan/17/china-population-decline-accelerates-as-birthrate-hits-record-low.
7. Tian Wang and Quanbao Jiang, "Recent trend and corelates of induced abortion in China: evidence from the 2017 China Fertility Survey," National Library of Medicine, November 24, 2022, https://www.ncbi.nlm.nih.gov/pmc/articles/PMC9700931/#:~:text=Between%202015%20and%202019%2C%20%20the,was%209.76%20million%20%5B4%5D.
8. Arpan Rai, "South Korea to create new ministry to tackle plummeting birth rate," Independent, May 9, 2024, https://ca.news.yahoo.com/south-korea-create-ministry-tackle-114621107.html
9. "The Lancet: World population likely to shrink after mid-century, forecasting major shifts in global population and economic power," IHME, July 14, 2020, https://www.healthdata.org/news-events/newsroom/news-releases/lancet-world-population-likely-shrink-after-mid-century.
10. "Population in more than 20 countries to halve by 2100: Study," Aljazeera, July 15, 2020, https://www.aljazeera.com/news/2020/7/15/population-in-more-than-20-countries-to-halve-by-2100-study.
11. "The Lancet: World population likely to shrink after mid-century, forecasting major shifts in global population and economic power," IHME,
12. Mariko Oi, "Asia is spending big to battle low birth rates - will it work?" BBC, May 16, 2023, https://www.bbc.com/news/business-65478376.
13. James Gallagher, "Fertility rate: 'Jaw-dropping' global crash in children being born," BBC, July 14, 2020, https://www.bbc.com/news/health-53409521.

14. Zhao Yimeng, "Govt aims to reduce costs associated with raising families," China Daily, April 9, 2024, https://www.chinadaily.com.cn/a/202404/09/WS66149919a31082fc043c0e66.html.
15. Oi, "Asia is spending big to battle low birth rates - will it work?" BBC.
16. Pablo Alvarez, "Charted: The World's Aging Population from 1950 to 2100," Visual Capitalist, May 29, 2023, https://www.visualcapitalist.com/cp/charted-the-worlds-aging-population-1950-to-2100/#:~:text=population%20across%20countries.-,The%20World's%20Aging%20Population%20from%201950%20to%202100,and%20eventually%2024%25%20by%202100.
17. Alvarez, "Charted: The World's Aging Population from 1950 to 2100," Visual Capitalist.
18. Pablo Alvarez, "What does the global decline of the fertility rate look like?" June 17, 2022, World Economic Forum, https://www.weforum.org/agenda/2022/06/global-decline-of-fertility-rates-visualised/.
19. Jenni Pettay and Robert Lynch, "Women in cities less likely to have children," *Behavioral Ecology,* March 18, 2021, 10.1093/beheco/arab007, Eurakalert, https://www.eurekalert.org/news-releases/661392.
20. Lyman Stone, "Higher Rent, Fewer Babies? Housing Costs and Fertility Decline," Institute for Family Studies, October 11, 2018, https://ifstudies.org/blog/higher-rent-fewer-babies-housing-costs-and-fertility-decline.
21. Jennie E Brand and Dwight Davis, "The impact of college education on fertility: evidence for heterogeneous effects," *Demography* vol. 48,3 (2011): 863-87, doi:10.1007/s13524-011-0034-3, https://www.ncbi.nlm.nih.gov/pmc/articles/PMC3449224/.
22. Norman P Li, et al, "Too materialistic to get married and have children?," *PloS one* vol. 10,5 e0126543. (May 8, 2015), doi:10.1371/journal.pone, https://www.ncbi.nlm.nih.gov/pmc/articles/PMC4425653/#:~:text=Thus%2C%20our%20Modified%20Incompatibility%20of,a%20lower%20number%20of%20children.
23. "4.5% of adults in the US identify as LGBT," Williams Institute, March 5, 2019, https://williamsinstitute.law.ucla.edu/press/lgbt-adults-us-press-release/.

24. "Steep decline in world fertility rates: contraceptive use up sharply," *Sozial- und Praventivmedizin* vol. 37,5 (1992): 254-5, https://pubmed.ncbi.nlm.nih.gov/1462719/#:~:text=The%20greatest%20development%20in%20reproductive,in%20a%20considerable%20fertility%20decline.
25. S D Mumford and E Kessel, "Role of abortion in control of global population growth," *Clinics in obstetrics and gynaecology* vol. 13,1 (1986): 19-31, https://pubmed.ncbi.nlm.nih.gov/3709011/.
26. H.S. Borji, "4 Global Economic Issues of an Aging Population," Investopedia, December 11, 2023, https://www.investopedia.com/articles/investing/011216/4-global-economic-issues-aging-population.asp#:~:text=Many%20industrialized%20nations%20are%20realizing,surge%20in%20health%20care%20costs.&text=The%20decline%20in%20the%20working,supply%20shortage%20of%20qualified%20workers.
27. Arturo Castellanos Canales, "Still More Room to Grow: Immigrants Can Reverse the U.S. Population Decline and Its Economic Consequences," January 29, 2024, National Immigration Forum, https://immigrationforum.org/article/still-more-room-to-grow-immigrants-can-reverse-the-u-s-population-decline-and-its-economic-consequences/#:~:text=Impacts%20of%20Low%20Population%-20Growth&text=Due%20to%20the%20slow%20population,in%20December%202023%20was%203.7%25.
28. Andrew Flowers, "The Great People Shortage Hits China," Business Insider, February 1, 2023, https://www.businessinsider.com/china-shrinking-population-worker-labor-shortage-grim-omen-global-economy-2023-2.
29. "Population in more than 20 countries to halve by 2100: Study," Aljazeera, July 15, 2020, https://www.aljazeera.com/news/2020/7/15/population-in-more-than-20-countries-to-halve-by-2100-study.
30. "The Lancet: World population likely to shrink after mid-century, forecasting major shifts in global population and economic power," IHME.

31. "Violence against women," World Health Organization, March 25, 2024, https://www.who.int/news-room/fact-sheets/detail/violence-against-women#:~:text=Estimates%20published%20by%20WHO%20indicate,violence%20is%20intimate%20partner%20violence.

Chapter 4: Africa's Prophetic Mandate: Delivering Christ's Message of Life to the World

1. Saifaddin Galal, "Population growth rate in Africa from 2000 to 2030," Statista, March 28, 2024, https://www.statista.com/statistics/1224179/population-growth-in-africa/#:~:text=In%202022%2C%20the%20total%20%20population,birth%2C%20the%20African%20population%20was.
2. "Population of Nigeria," The World Counts, accessed June 2, 2024, https://www.theworldcounts.com/populations/countries/nigeria.
3. "2022 Report on International Freedom: Kenya," U.S. Department of State, accessed June 2, 2024, https://www.state.gov/reports/2022-report-on-international-religious-freedom/%20kenya/#:~:text=Religious%20Demography,-The%20U.S.%20%20government&text=The%20government%20estimates%20that%20%20as,to%20various%20traditional%20religious%20beliefs.
4. Chara Scroope, "South African Culture," Cultural Atlas, 2019, https://culturalatlas.sbs.com.au/south-african-culture/south-african-culture-religion.
5. Life Equip Global, https://lifeequipglobal.org/.
6. "Respect for Unborn Human Life: The Church's Constant Teaching," United States Conference of Catholic Bishops, accessed June 2, 2024, https://www.usccb.org/issues-and-action/human-life-and-dignity/abortion/respect-for-unborn-human-life.

Chapter 5: Marriage: The Covenant for Life

1. "The Covenant of Marriage: Truth That Can Transform Your Marriage," Precept Austin, August 7, 2023, https://www.preceptaustin.org/the_covenant_of_marriage.

2. Carolina Aragão, "Among young adults without children, men are more likely than women to say they want to be parents someday," Pew Research Center, February 15, 2024, https://www.pewresearch.org/short-reads/2024/02/15/among-young-adults-without-children-men-are-more-likely-than-women-to-say-they-want-to-be-parents-someday/.
3. Aragão, "Among young adults without children, men are more likely than women to say they want to be parents someday," Pew Research Center.

Chapter 6: Be Fruitful: The Divine Call to Multiply
1. Ronald Rolheiser, *The Holy Longing: A Search for a Christian Spirituality* (New York: Image, 2014), 199.
2. "Unintended Pregnancy and Abortion Worldwide," Guttmacher, March 2022, https://www.guttmacher.org/fact-sheet/induced-abortion-worldwide.
3. "Abortion," World Health Organization, May 17, 2024, https://www.who.int/news-room/fact-sheets/detail/abortion.
4. Ida Peréa Monteiro, et al, "Prevalence of sexually transmissible infections in adolescents treated in a family planning outpatient clinic for adolescents in the western Amazon," PloS One vol. 18,6 e0287633 (June 23, 2023), doi:10.1371/journal.pone.0287633, https://www.ncbi.nlm.nih.gov/pmc/articles/PMC10289307/#:~:text=The%20yearly%20incidence%20estimated%20by,common%20in%20women%20%5B1%5D.
5. "Ending Sexual Violence," Equality Now, accessed June 3, 2024, https://equalitynow.org/end_sexual_violence/.
6. Antra Bhatt, "Expert's take: By undercounting single mothers, we underserve families," UN Women, February 11, 2020, https://www.unwomen.org/en/news/stories/2020/2/experts-take-antra-bhatt-on-single-parent-households.
7. "Commercial Sexual Exploitation," GFEMS, accessed June 3, 2024, https://gfems.org/modern-slavery/issues/about-commercial-sexual-exploitation/.

8. Jannik Lindner, "Pornography Industry Statistics [Fresh Research]," Gitnux, January 9, 2024, https://gitnux.org/pornography-industry-statistics/#:~:text=The%20global%20pornography%20industry%20is,engine%20requests%20are%20pornography%2Drelated.

Chapter 7: Choices and Consequences: The Hidden Realities of Abortion Methods

1. Marge Berer, "Abortion Law and Policy Around the World: In Search of Decriminalization," *Health and human rights* vol. 19,1 (2017): 13-27, https://www.ncbi.nlm.nih.gov/pmc/articles/PMC5473035/.
2. Serhii Pyvovarov and Yevhen Spirin, "Abortions were legalized (again) in the USSR 68 years ago. Their number grew to seven million a year, but sex education remained at the level of a biology textbook," Babel, November 29, 2023, https://babel.ua/en/texts/55076-abortions-were-legalized-again-in-the-ussr-68-years-ago-their-number-grew-to-seven-million-a-year-but-sex-education-remained-at-the-level-of-a-biology-textbook-how-it-was-in-archival-photos.
3. "Law and Policy Guide: Life Exceptions," Center for Reproductive Rights, accessed April 9, 2024, https://reproductiverights.org/maps/worlds-abortion-laws/law-and-policy-guide-life-exceptions/#:~:text=Nearly%2090%25%20of%20countries%20worldwide,cases%20of%20rape%20or%20incest.
4. Danielle B. Cooper and Gary W. Menefee, "Dilation and Curettage," National Library of Medicine, May 7, 2023, https://www.ncbi.nlm.nih.gov/books/NBK568791/.
5. "Dilation and Evacuation (D&E) Surgery Overview," Kaiser Permanente, November 27, 2023, https://healthy.kaiserpermanente.org/health-wellness/health-encyclopedia/he.dilation-and-evacuation-d-e.tw2462.
6. "Medication Abortion: Your Questions Answered," Yale Medicine, September 11, 2023, https://www.yalemedicine.org/news/medication-abortion-your-questions-answered.
7. Annie Stuart, "Levonorgestrel Emergency Contraception: Plan B," WebMD, March 12, 2023, https://www.webmd.com/sex/birth-control/plan-b.

8. Susan Wills, "New Studies Show All Emergency Contraceptives Can Cause Early Abortion," Charlotte Lozier Institute, January 1, 2014, https://lozierinstitute.org/emergencycontraceptive.
9. Hannah Howard, "Medical and Social Risks Associated with Unmitigated Distribution of Mifepristone: A Primer," Charlotte Lozier Institute, October 1, 2020, https://lozierinstitute.org/medical-and-social-risks-associated-with-unmitigated-distribution-of-mifepristone-a-primer/.
10. Carmen Ciganda and Amalia Laborde, "Herbal infusions used for induced abortion," Clinical Toxicology 41(3) (2003): 235-39, https://pubmed.ncbi.nlm.nih.gov/12807304/.
11. "Trauma in pregnancy: a unique challenge," Mayo Clinic, October 6, 2017, https://www.mayoclinic.org/medical-professionals/trauma/news/trauma-in-pregnancy-a-unique-challenge/mac-20431356#:~:text=Force%20from%20trauma%20can%20sheer,fetal%20loss%2C%22%20says%20Dr.
12. "Douching: Don't Do It Despite These Common Myths," All About Women, accessed June 4, 2024, https://www.allaboutwomenmd.com/knowledge-center/douching.html.
13. L Lewis Wall and Awol Yemane, "Infectious Complications of Abortion," National Library of Medicine, November 23, 2022, https://www.ncbi.nlm.nih.gov/pmc/articles/PMC9683598/.
14. "Unsafe abortion: A preventable danger," Doctors Without Borders, March 7, 2019, https://www.doctorswithoutborders.org/latest/unsafe-abortion-preventable-danger.
15. Carlson B. Sama, Leopold Ndemnge Aminde, and Fru F. Angwafo III, "Clandestine abortion causing uterine perforation and bowel infarction in a rural area: a case report and brief review," BMC Research Notes, February 16, 2016, https://bmcresnotes.biomedcentral.com/articles/10.1186/s13104-016-1926-5#:~:text=Perforation%20of%20the%20uterus%2C%20bleeding,to%20intraperitoneal%20hemorrhage%20and%20septicemia.
16. B Barnett, "Youth often risk unsafe abortions," National Library of Medicine, October 1993, https://pubmed.ncbi.nlm.nih.gov/12287144/.

17. David C. Reardon, "The abortion and mental health controversy: A comprehensive literature review of common ground agreements, disagreements, actionable recommendations, and research opportunities," National Library of Medicine, October 29, 2018, https://www.ncbi.nlm.nih.gov/pmc/articles/PMC6207970/.
18. "Unsafe abortion incidence and mortality," World Health Organization, accessed June 4, 2024, https://iris.who.int/bitstream/

Printed in the USA
CPSIA information can be obtained
at www.ICGtesting.com
CBHW070031190724
11796CB00025B/1149